## ADVANCE PRAISE FOR *FOOTBALL SISSY*

"Jack's sports reporting was always fair, honest and straightforward. He tells his own story in the same exact way."
—**Cris Collinsworth**, NBC *Sunday Night Football*

"*Football Sissy* traces a fascinating path through two lives—one public, one intensely private. I hope Jack telling his story helps five, ten, twenty-five people in the macho orbit of professional sports to think, 'It's okay to be different—and I'm not going to live in the shadows anymore.'"
—**Peter King**, four-time National Sportswriter of the Year

"Back in his football days, Jack Brennan was perpetually the most delightful person in the room. None of us knew that he had a secret that he was deathly afraid to share. Now, in his own inimitable, hilarious and courageous style, he's sharing that secret and letting us inside his world and the world of professional football."
—**Joe Posnanski**, author of *New York Times* bestseller
*The Baseball 100*

"This is fearlessly honest stuff from a great human who went through things I never knew about. I admire him all the more for telling this story."
—**Phil Simms**, Super Bowl XXI MVP

JACK BRENNAN

# FOOTBALL
# *Sissy*

## A CROSS-DRESSING MEMOIR

Belt Publishing

First Edition 2025

ISBN 9781540270047

Belt Publishing

6101 Penn Avenue, Suite 201

Pittsburgh, PA 15206

www.beltpublishing.com

Cover art by David Wilson

Book design by Julie Foster

# CONTENTS

# PREFACE

A great friend of mine for almost forty years, a colleague in newspaper sportswriting before I moved to the National Football League, always thought I was terribly funny—but weird. I could get Bill Koch laughing so hard over lunch that his Diet Coke would drip out his nose. Upon recovering, he'd sputter, "Chief...you ain't right."

And every time, I'd think, *Chief, if you only knew even the half of it.*

But I kept Bill in the dark. No one could ever find out about me, and especially not him, my other male buds, or anyone in the NFL. I feared an existential loss, the forfeiture of male camaraderie. Lunches, tennis, or a few beers would never be the same, if they continued at all. I dreaded no longer fitting in with the discourse of men about sports, politics, and women.

Working for thirty-four years in Cincinnati, I always had a public-facing job in very masculine fields. I was a pro football journalist, then briefly a baseball reporter, then a pro football scribe again, and finally the public relations director of the NFL Bengals. I was my newspaper's main beat man for a Bengals Super Bowl team and a Reds World Series winner, and for twenty-four years with the Bengals I was the gatekeeper for local and national media seeking access to players and coaches. I was occasionally an interview subject myself, and I was on the contacts lists of people across the country. I feared that I was especially vulnerable to a widespread stir should embarrassing revelations about me arise.

Like—just for an example—the revelation that I was a closeted cross-dresser, a guy with a visceral urge to play-act as a woman in skirts and heels and makeup. Queer men like me were presumed to not exist in the NFL world, and particularly in a team's "football side" jobs, the ones requiring daily contact with half-dressed or undressed players in locker rooms and clubhouses. The air was heavy with an unspoken implication that in the NFL inner sanctum, queers should not exist.

Inside the locker room, you'd hear occasional gossip about some players being closeted gays. Everyone knew that a handful of players had come out as gay after retirement. And sometimes one would hear a gay slur, though usually uttered more casually than vitriolically.

But away from the locker room, inside football-side departments like public relations, athletic training, team logistics, and equipment management, the idea that all of us were razor-straight was no less a given than that we hailed from Earth instead of Mars. If you're here, you're not a queer, the walls seemed to say.

Old-time football culture was at the root of this shutout of LGBTQ+ expression. The sport's very DNA held that queer guys were anathema to toughness and winning chemistry. Possibly a team could have abided a lesbian athletic trainer—possibly one already had, without fanfare—but woe be the squad whose football side tried to abide the softness of a male sissy.

The NFL's New York main office was generally a shade to the left on social issues, leading the league's staunchly conservative franchise owners by the nose to the reality that mild progressivism was smart business. As a brand, the NFL strongly supported PR campaigns for causes like Hispanic heritage awareness and breast cancer research, and in 2014 it responded to questions about possible future self-proclaimed gay players by proclaiming itself a "football meritocracy" where sexual orientation would not be among the factors determining success or failure. I took the initiative to modify the league statement into an individual one for the Bengals, and club owner Mike Brown agreed it should be kept on file. But this outlook did not trickle far down into the daily operations of individual teams.

For a decade before joining the Bengals, I belonged to the national fraternity of media covering the NFL. There wasn't an "out" queer person among us. Males, measuring maybe 95 percent of the group, had to be perceived as tolerably straight and tough to function in the locker room atmosphere.

But in 2021, at age sixty-eight, some four years into my retirement, I spilled at least the barest bones of my story. I offered it to Joe Posnanski, a nationally acclaimed writer friend, who published it in *The Athletic*. And now, some four years later, comes this book.

I've never suffered acute guilt or shame about sometimes wanting to feel like a girl and wanting others, even if just playfully, to treat me as one. I have felt transitory shame on specific occasions, but it has never been a deep shame that wouldn't pass. I've never felt "wrong to the core" inside, never thought I was more messed up in areas that really matter than the average human. But I know that even socially progressive people have been prone to think of closeted cross-dressers as rather pathetic, lacking the unapologetically bold quality of performing drag queens.

Cross-dressing "could hardly have a worse reputation," says a thoughtful unbylined essay titled "The Psychology of Cross-Dressing" on the School of Life website. "The concept of a man taking pleasure in putting on a pair of stockings seems laughable, pitiful—and plain sinister."

Known for short as "CDs," cross-dressers are on the transgender (TG) spectrum, but we are not "transsexuals" or drag queens, as I understand the terms.

We don't desire gender-altering surgery. We don't feel we were "born in the wrong body"; we just want to wear the wrong clothes, not 24/7 but regularly. We are comfortable enough owning our primary identity as males.

We share that male identity, I think, with drag queens. But to me, drag queens seem not to fully care whether they "pass." Rather, a drag queen dresses to be real as a man adopting female expression in a flashy and fearless way. When I dress, though I know I won't fully pass, I aspire to subsume myself in a 100 percent female projection and persona. I want to be mistaken for a glamorous and totally made-up Fox News anchor babe. I want to be desired by men to no less a degree than Helen of Troy.

I don't personally much care whether you call me "he" or "she." Though it's fun to be accorded the female pronoun, I know what I am— a male in female garb—and that's even part of the sizzle for me. Sometimes I'd even prefer "he." But I've been around CDs who were most uncomfortable with male pronouns, and of course their wishes should be respected.

Despite societal advances in parts of the planet, the premise that queer folks are inherently disordered still conditions almost all of us. Mind-bending cruelty toward LGBTQ+ people, after all, has had a three-thousand-year head start on understanding and respect. Even urbane and progressive folks face a struggle to rise above the myths that have warped and frightened us.

And cross-dressers, lonely souls, are often looked down upon even in comparison with other queers. We feel shame about our identities—unlike those proud drag queens—and this makes us particularly vulnerable to hits from patriarchy and misogyny.

Perhaps my CD nature was the basis of the quirkiness Bill Koch always found in my sense of humor. For sure, my compulsion has put me through experiences you won't see bragged about on Facebook. Some of the history recounted here reads as so oddball, even to me, that I laugh to think it really could have happened that way.

But it's all true and, upon full consideration, not entirely funny. There's a toll from spending every day since age three—the first time I felt the urge to cross-dress—with background worry over who might find out. No human should have to carry that baggage of shame.

I am of course but one among zillions who have suffered for the sin of sexual nonconformity, and so many have been wronged so much more profoundly than me. Lost jobs. Lost families. Lost lives. So I hope the attempted laughs in this story, along with parts that might discomfit the buttoned-up sides of straight men, will further awareness that queer people are not so different from "normal" as the majority may think.

You can be fully respectful and inclusive of queers—going so far as to jump for joy when your child announces same-sex marriage plans—but if you're among those content with a sex life flaunting no major conventions, you can't dodge the conditioning that queers will always stand apart from you in a starkly defining way. It's the right vs. wrong, black vs. white, no middle ground way of King Heterosexuality on our planet.

I was lucky enough to roll into retirement with a Regular Guy life that blocked all but my tiny inner circle from knowing about me. I have an amazing wife of nearly fifty years—Valerie—and three adult children plus two granddaughters. I played high school football and scads of recreational sports, and I am about as hairy as a *Homo sapiens* gets. So I knew it would rock many to learn that I also had an unstoppable urge to be the sexiest girl in the room.

But I also knew that I didn't want to keep such a huge part of my life a secret, even if others wished that I would. When I told my sister Andrea's husband, Frank, whom I love dearly, his initial reaction clearly was disappointment.

"I'm not sure why you're telling me this," he said one evening when Valerie and I were visiting their home in Atlanta. His hands were on his hips, and his demeanor was from a spot somewhere between pissed off and crestfallen.

"I don't know that I wanted or needed this knowledge," he went on. "Maybe sometimes we don't need to know everything. Maybe it's better to spare people from all of our revelations."

It was a classic request to a queer for self-censoring, and I didn't blame him. In the culture that reared Frank and most of the rest of us, queers were expected to accept being shamed into silence, as their very existence was considered awkward and uncomfortable. But this was a good exercise for me, since I expected to encounter others who would react this way.

"Frank, I love you," I said, "but this is not about you or your own safe space. Much as you might think you'd have preferred blissful ignorance, that's not a fair ask from anyone, not if I choose to own this side of myself."

"I'm still not sure why you have to be so forward with it," he said.

"We all deserve the comfort of being whole with others, especially the people we love," I said, "and if you ask me how I enjoyed my weekend, I shouldn't have to lie or dissemble if I spent part of it cross-dressing."

Frank is a good man, and his body language softened as I went on. He would become, in a very short time, much more comfortable with my fully expressed self. The discomfort I caused him gave way to a greater connection between us, because I risked vulnerability.

I'm aware that many smart and otherwise well-informed readers will confess to having thought very little about cross-dressing, and to understanding even less. It surely is among the least discussed areas of gender and sexual expression, and I hope this book can spread some light and insight. But I also wish to make clear that I know my attraction to dresses and makeup affords me no platform to speak for women. I don't identify as a woman, and I don't claim to understand the vast part of a woman's experience. I realize that my fantasies about traditional female beauty are in large measure the cultural product of an imposed patriarchy, and that they are justly resented by plenty of women. My CD self is much more about costuming than culture, and I actively seek to avoid erecting a soapbox on anyone else's turf.

Conversely, others cannot tell me what does or should turn me on, presuming I am involving only myself or other consenting adults. As Dr. Fred Berlin, director of the Johns Hopkins Sex and Gender Clinic, told *The New York Times* in 2019, "People don't choose what arouses them—they discover it." Ergo, I claim the right to express my feelings as a male drawn to gender-bending. The opinions and experiences related here are from that source and no other.

I sometimes self-identify as a "sissy" because my fantasies involve being ultra girly and submissive to men. But when I got some of my very earliest feedback on this book, gay friends very dear to me applied serious pushback to my use of "sissy" in the title and manuscript. They said it was too degrading and that reading it gave them bad vibes.

"You are not a sissy!" a male friend said with considerable emotion. "You are strong and bold and funny. That word is just so hurtful. It has been used for so long to devalue and humiliate people. It has been used against me."

So I looked up "sissy" in my Webster's Collegiate, and indeed, it terms the word a "disparaging and offensive" way to refer to an effeminate boy or man. But I have always called myself a sissy, perhaps as a way of taking on society's scorn and finding that I can stand it. In consideration of my friends' feedback, I have tried to be sparing with the term, but I can't excise it completely from a book about myself.

It just wouldn't be genuine.

Jack Brennan
Cincinnati, Ohio
October 2024

## CHAPTER 0

# HOW DID I GET HERE?

From inside my front door, I can see so many flashing lights it's blinding. And unfortunately, it's all because of me. I'm suspected of being a burglar or home invader, so this time the jig is really up. There will be no escape.

Not an escape from criminal charges, I mean, as no crime has occurred. The misunderstanding can be cleared up soon enough. The awful thing, the grisly thing there's no escaping from, is that I'm wearing stilettos, short shorts, a silky blonde wig, and a slinky tank top draping my voluptuous silicone breasts. This version of myself is not who my neighbors and local police know, but damned if they won't all get clued in muy pronto, due to this three-cop-car commotion.

It was stupefying to conceive this could be happening. To the little boy feeling quite alone in the world, dazed over his sudden lust for puffed sleeves, such a situation would have been inconceivable in any sense. The eleven-year-old hooking up his mother's garters certainly never foresaw it, and ditto for the twenty-year-old driven to don a bra behind a closed door in a fraternity house. And again, it wasn't so much about facing a slew of police with guns drawn. The bigger part—the truly unimaginable part— would have been my going out to meet anyone, anywhere, dressed as I was.

But this was my sudden reality on a July night at age fifty-one. So I took a deep breath and stepped onto my front porch.

## CHAPTER I

# YES (LADY GAGA), I WAS BORN THIS WAY

Wanting to dress like a girl is among my earliest memories. In the fall of 1955, growing up in Dallas, Texas, at about age three and a half, I was taken by my mother on what would prove a landmark visit to some neighbors. Their daughter Janie (not her real name) was about my age, and while our moms were chatting, Janie and I went to play in her room.

This was not the first time we had gotten together in this way, but this playdate came with a new twist. Janie's blouse had just the cutest puffed sleeves, and I became entranced by it. I wanted to know what it would feel like to wear it.

Check that. I already had a damn good idea how it would feel, and I wanted to *experience* it. I wanted to gaze at a new self in the mirror and then put on a complete girl's outfit and be seen in it by others.

At three and a half, I didn't question or analyze my feelings. I just acted, suggesting to Janie that we swap tops.

She happily agreed, and when we went in to show our moms, they reacted as if it were just the silliness of small children. But while I giggled on the outside, my heart was pounding. I knew I had uncovered something powerful. I didn't want to take off that blouse, and when Janie made clear that dress-up time was over, I felt regret. I suddenly had little enthusiasm for our normal play. While switching back to my own shirt, I had visions of walking in our neighborhood with that blouse on, for any and all neighbors to see. How exciting such a stroll would be!

But I knew even as I fantasized that this could never actually happen. Boys were simply never to do such things. (A huge reason it was so exciting!) It quickly dawned on me that I had a secret I could never reveal to anyone. Though I didn't feel inner shame, accepting myself with surprising ease, I knew the world would think otherwise. It would be nothing short of catastrophic to give anyone even an inkling.

With this dose of reality, my urges would not be front and center again for some years. Plenty of other things interested me as I progressed into my preteen years, and playing with dolls and tea sets was not among them. I loved toy trucks and toy guns and "army men," and I developed a passionate interest in sports. I played on the sandlot level almost every day—softball, basketball, and tackle football without pads.

As I grew older, I watched big-time sports on TV and read about them daily. I spent almost all my allowance on baseball and football cards, and my school classes came to know me as their resident expert on sports news. It was a fine kid's life. I had plenty of friends, all boys, and that intense day at Janie's was…heck, I didn't know exactly what it was, but it didn't prey on my mind.

The desire to dress, though, would not remain dormant indefinitely. It next popped out, in a veiled way, when I reached fifth grade and entered a prep school whose uniforms included neckties. Outwardly I expressed disgust, professing that ties were for wimpy kids. But quietly I came to like being a "dress-up boy." I often enjoyed keeping my tie on during late-day periods when the dress code wasn't enforced and peers were shedding their cravats. I tended to obsess over the tie and adjust it almost constantly, making sure it looked perfect. I didn't make the mental connection to cross-dressing at the time, but I see it clearly now as a substitute.

By about age twelve, a boy's necktie was no longer enough. Old enough to be home alone, I went rummaging through my mom's things. Hers were the only ones available, as my only sister was out of high school and in a Catholic convent.

Mom was no fashionista, but she had plenty of stuff that interested me, particularly lingerie and hosiery. I loved putting on stockings and attaching them to a garter belt. (Is there anything in the world so completely feminine as a garter belt?) Sometimes I'd do hose and garters even when my parents were home. I'd slip them on in the bathroom, then pull up my pants and go about usual business. I would be inwardly very excited, feeling delicious tension over the outline of the garter being visible under my pants. But no one ever professed to notice, and I never felt remorse when my little show was over. I knew I just would keep doing it and keep hiding it.

These were also my first times dabbling with makeup. There was lipstick, of course, but what I remember most was the mascara, which was not at all like mascaras of today. It came in a tiny squeeze tube, like ointment, and you applied it with a separate brush, squirting it onto the brush like black toothpaste.

So primitive, but for me it was like dynamite. I marveled at how each stroke made my lashes long and alluring. I got a tingle from just the word *mascara*. It was a word a regular boy would certainly never speak, thus it just sounded so feminine.

Was Mom finding clues of my activities? I worried that she might notice a slip not folded right, or runs in her stockings, or that the mascara tube was running low rather quickly. But she never evinced such a concern.

Unquestionably, my parents were the wellspring of my freedom from deep recrimination about dressing. Not that they knew about it and handled it perfectly—I'm sure they were totally in the dark, as I felt I needed them to be—but the key was that I simply received the loving care that should be every child's birthright from two good people living the conventional white heartland life of the mid-twentieth century.

Some kids would later say that my folks were too easy on me, and they once said it quite bitterly. When I was sixteen-ish, I was caught egging unlucky cars at Southern Methodist University with some guys. When we were serving our sentence (washing police cars for four consecutive Saturday mornings), the other guys were complaining about their punishments at home.

"I'm totally grounded for twelve weeks," one proclaimed.

"I can't even go to basketball practice for two weeks," another said. "I might as well quit the team."

"God, did my dad scream at me," shuddered a third. "The neighbors heard it."

Then it was my turn.

"Well, my mom and dad made me feel pretty bad," I said. "But they really seemed more sad than mad. They just said it was so disappointing I would do that. They're kind of acting cold to me right now."

"That's it?" said one. "You're not even grounded? They're 'cold' to you? That is such bullshit!"

This proved to be a consensus opinion, and for a few days I was literally ostracized.

But maybe my folks' disappointment was punishment enough for me. Maybe draconian discipline was not always the way to go. I knew my folks still loved me and were willing to give me a second chance. Ted and Helen Brennan certainly had their struggles—Dad died a severe alcoholic and Mom suffered late in life from a bipolar disorder—but their trust helped imbue me with durable self-esteem. I never was made to feel unworthy of all the love they could muster, and they mustered plenty despite their issues. Their unconditional love made me know I was still a great kid, even if I was a convicted egger and a secret sissy.

## CHAPTER 2

# DAD HAD A PROBLEM

D ad provided the initial spark for my love of sports. He had made our flat and treeless backyard the spot for neighborhood softball long before I was old enough to play. He never put pressure on me to excel or always win at any sport. He just enjoyed the sports experience as a fan and a father. Sports were always fun with Dad, never a burden as a participant and always the very best regarding spectator opportunities.

His finest hour in the spectator category came in late December of 1966, when I was fourteen and desperate for a ticket to the January 1 NFL championship game between the Cowboys and the Packers at the Dallas Cotton Bowl. A ticket in this era was far more precious than younger readers may realize, because until 1973, crazy as it now sounds, home games of NFL teams were blacked out in their own TV markets even when the games were sellouts. Avid fans who couldn't get tickets would rent motel rooms outside the blackout radius—usually about a seventy-five-mile drive—to access the telecast. But we didn't know anyone doing that, so a ticket was my only chance to experience this monumentally important contest beyond the limited realm of radio.

"I know you won't like this idea," I told Mom and Dad, "but I need to camp out at the Cowboys office next Thursday night. The last of the tickets are on sale Friday morning, and I can get back to school in the afternoon somehow. I'll have no shot unless I'm in line overnight. It can be my main Christmas present, please!"

By 1966 standards, it was a very expensive ticket. Ten bucks.

Ted and Helen declined an immediate decision, driving me crazy as the crucial Thursday approached. But on Tuesday, Dad came home from work with an envelope.

"I figured you'd like to have these," he said.

Inside were two tickets to the game. He had scored them from a business contact. I already knew he had connections for college tickets—we had gone to many big games together—but I had never dreamed he could do it for Dallas's first-ever hosting of the NFL championship. He said he didn't need to go himself, so I could invite a friend.

I'd like to say that Dad and I hugged and kissed, but he wasn't one to show a lot of emotion or physical affection. Dad did give me great back scratches—a part of his repertoire that he started years before with my brother—and he had a great sense of humor. When Mom would try to impose unreasonable conditions on something Dad and I were planning, he'd sometimes wink at me and whisper, "Let's don't [do it] and say we did." He knew that kids were meant to have good times.

But there was, of course, through it all, Dad's alcoholism.

I grew up with unquestioning acceptance that Dad and Mom would drink after dinner—usually "highballs," bourbon with club soda—and sometimes Dad would fall asleep in his chair before going to bed. I knew no other life, and it didn't seem a bad one. But as I moved into my high school years, the only one of the three kids still living at home, Dad's disease worsened.

"I'm goin' to the K of C for a swim. You wanna go?" Dad asked me that late on a summer Saturday afternoon when I was fourteen. It was just a few months before he would score me those priceless Cowboys tickets. The "K of C" was the Knights of Columbus, a Catholic men's organization about three miles from home with a lodge house and swimming pool.

I was game for the trip, knowing I'd get not only a swim but a Dad-funded burger and fries from the lodge house grill. Though I knew by this time that Dad sometimes drank too much at night and liked "a cold Bud" with lunch on weekends, I didn't suspect anything amiss. But less than two blocks out of our driveway I was screaming "Look out!" because Dad had narrowly missed swerving into a parked car. He was seriously drunk, that cold Bud clearly having led to three or four more.

"I saw it," Dad declared about the parked car. And he said nothing more.

Nor did I. Nothing like this had ever happened, and I was not up to flatly telling him he was unfit to drive. We had never opened up about his drinking as a family, even when an acolyte from his office would deliver him home to us after a binge. I sat in terrified silence until we approached busy Abrams Road.

"Please slow d—!" I started to yell before the stop sign. But I was too late. Dad lunged into the divided six-lane thoroughfare with only a cursory tap on the brakes and prompted two blaring honks as he made a crazy wide left turn into traffic.

No driver made an attempt to intervene or follow, however, and of course there were no cell phones to call the cops. Dad was unrestrained on the streets, with me as his frantic copilot.

"Don't you want to turn here?"

I was trying to get him off Abrams, onto an alternate route we had recently discovered. It was a wide residential through street, offering space as well as less traffic. He made the turn, and the next three minutes were not so bad. We came really close to only one parked car, and the two kids on bikes that we saw were coming toward us, well on the other side of the street.

But in just another moment I had to shout, "You've gotta be real careful here!" The K of C building was blessedly in sight, but between us and safety lay the cataract of Northwest Highway, a city-spanning route twice as busy as Abrams.

I feared we might bite it at this point, but we found Northwest miraculously clear of traffic. Dad made it into the left turn lane and swerved his way into the K of C lot.

I tried to swim a little while Dad went into the bar. I hoped, naively, that he might sober up. But after about twenty minutes, someone from the staff waved me out of the pool.

"Your dad needs a ride home," the man told me. "Can someone come and get you both? You can use the phone in the bar. It's OK if you need to leave his car here overnight."

Perhaps I should have been more upset and embarrassed, but now that Dad and I weren't in acute danger of dying in an auto accident, a detached stoicism took over. It would prove to be an emotional harbor I would use often in the coming years when Dad had his "incidents."

It was an extraordinary thing to have to deal with, but the way I saw it, people everywhere were dealing with other extraordinary and unfair things every day. They weren't dissolving in a pool of self-pity, and I would not, I determined, let this fuck up all the good things in my life.

Mom had been out of the house when Dad and I left. Now I was able to reach her.

"Oh honey, I'm so sorry you are having to deal with this," she said. "I guess I shouldn't have left the house today. He hasn't been right since he came home from that business trip to Houston on Thursday. They had some kind of a banquet, and those things set him off. I knew he drank way too much yesterday. I thought this morning he seemed better, but…"

"So what do we do now?"

"I'll come get you, and then I'll see if Jim Culberson can take me back there to get his car."

Culberson was the guy at Dad's insurance company who'd occasionally bring Dad home from binges. Jim was a devil-may-care claims adjuster, prone to getting into scrapes, but Dad as claims manager would always protect him from the big bosses. Jim loved Dad and would do anything for him.

Twenty minutes later, Mom was at the K of C to get us.

"I don't want to go into the bar," she said. "I think that would upset him. Can you go in? Get some help getting him out to the car if you can."

That mission accomplished, I was then alone at home with Dad for an hour while Mom and Culberson retrieved his car. It didn't matter; he was asleep in their bedroom. He spent all of Sunday in the bedroom, Mom and I agreeing he was probably too ashamed to be with us, and he was not so far gone at this point that he didn't realize he had to sober up for work. By Monday, the household was back to normal. The three of us didn't talk about it anymore.

And that's how it went for the rest of my high school years. Dad would be OK most of the time, the normal Dad I loved, but a couple times a year, he'd go off the deep end. Culberson would bring him home, or maybe he'd make it by himself somehow, and after a couple days of sadness and tension, we'd be back on track as a family until the next time. My brother Pete had moved to Colorado, and my sister Andrea was in the convent, and though they knew of the situation and showed concern, it was Mom and I who had to deal with it—until I went off to college at eighteen and Mom was largely left on her own.

I was no longer even in Texas in March of '76 when Mom called to tell us Dad had died. We would never know the exact day, because he was found by Culberson in a cheap motel room that he'd checked into four days previously.

He was only sixty-six. Mom lived until 1995, passing at eighty-one in Cincinnati, a few days after suffering a stroke. I was way too deep in the closet to ever consider coming out to either of them, and I'm positive Dad never had an inkling. Mom didn't seem to, either, but she did come awfully close once to finding me out.

# THE CD LIFE: CLOTHES

I like dressing pretty, in pastel pink over a delicate pale yellow.

I like dressing frilly, in lace and buttons and bows.

I like dressing sexy, in shiny blouses and slinky dresses and anything that shows a lot of skin.

I like dressing cute, in a snug jean skirt and a clingy top that shows off a great figure.

And thanks to my build, I can do it all by shopping at regular women's clothing stores. Tolerably fit at five-foot-ten and 165 pounds, with a women's shoe size of ten, I am just small enough to find a decent selection of gorgeous things in my size.

My favorite stores are Nordstrom Rack, Target, and Macy's. All three have very good clearance sections, and that's important, because I confess to having supported fast fashion, craving variety without breaking the bank. Some markdowns—like a shiny red short jacket with silver zippers that I found for $13 at Target—are just stupendous values. That jacket looks awesome over the fierce little silver-studded jean skirt I got also at Target, for *six bucks*. That skirt was so great-looking on the rack and so cheap, it didn't matter that I was wearing male clothes and not in a position to try on different sizes. I just bought two, a size ten and a twelve. Both fit, but I much prefer the tighter wrap of the ten.

Getting girl clothes to fit can be frustrating. A tank top can fit great just about everywhere but not cover my breasts well enough when tucked in tightly. Not that I'd shy from some cleavage—I'd die for it, actually—but great as my silicone breast forms are, they don't pass for real skin. But I still wear tanks often, and though I'll often freak out just as it's time to leave the house, I'll forget about it soon enough and find that in photos the fake boobs are adequately masked. In later years I've also discovered the sexiness of flimsy tops that drape over the bust without being tucked, covering my boobs just fine.

I'm a reasonably slim chick below my broad male shoulders, and though I often wish for a female's hips and butt, my shortcomings in those spots make it easier to fit into shorts, skirts, and jeans. I bought a pair of shorts in size small not long ago and wound up wishing I'd searched harder for an XS!

My belly and waist are slim enough that I sometimes wear crop tops, and it is one spectacular feeling to show that expanse of skin just above my belly button. It's an area I never dreamed of being able to expose for years, because Valerie wasn't ready for me to be that shaved. I suck it in like crazy for photos. With a regular top, tucked in, I'll usually be wearing two corsets, on which I've yanked the laces tight with savage determination. I use two because my favored Hollywood Dream Waist Cincher (by Frederick's of Hollywood) doesn't cover all the ground between my chest and my crotch. When I wasp-waist it up high with just one, trying to make my breasts stick out as much as possible, I'll be pooching out badly at tummy level. So I tie up another cincher to handle that bulge. That feeling of being tightly bound up is sexy, as I think plenty of people know.

And it's not really clothes, but I have to brag on one little bracelet I got for a buck at Claire's. It's pink and rubberized, and amid a sprinkling of little white hearts, it has the word "his" playfully printed in black. What a thing for a guy to wear.

## CHAPTER 3

# ALL ABOUT MOM

**A**s a kid, I never feared my folks would go nuts if they found out about me. They'd be devastated, of course, and it would be terribly sad for all, but I knew that unlike some queer kids, I wouldn't get kicked out of the house. Ted and Helen would support me as best they could figure out.

In the end my avid secrecy would spare them that grim task, but there was indeed one night—I think I was about thirteen—when Mom came perilously close to being forced to take it on.

"Honey, are you all right in there?"

Holy shit, she was standing right outside the bathroom door, barely forty-eight inches from me as I replaced her mascara and lipstick in a cupboard just inside the door. Only seconds before, I had just finished a painstaking application of said cosmetics.

"Haven't you been in there sort of a long time?" Mom asked. "If you're constipated..."

Great God Almighty, she was starting to actually open the door. No, I hadn't locked it, nor had I even pulled it completely shut. I had felt I was safe enough, with Mom reading in the other room, Dad away on a business trip, and my siblings already living elsewhere. Locking or even fully closing the door, I had deemed, would look too suspicious were Mom to pass by.

Bad plan, in hindsight. Nothing short of disastrous, it seemed at that moment. I would be caught in makeup, and despite my baseline confidence that I wouldn't be disowned, this was still mid-1960s Texas. Our sweetly conventional household would certainly never be quite the same again. My sissiness would prove to be the cause of tears, hand-wringing, and hushed parental conferences. "What are we going to do with our son?" they would ask themselves over and over.

This awful process of discovery, shock, and unpredictable repercussions would begin in a matter of just seconds…

The clunk was what saved me. As Mom kept pushing the door farther in, it bumped loudly against the cupboard door that I had just opened, causing Mom to pause and providing the precious seconds I needed.

"No, I'm fine!" I said, attempting urgency without hysteria. "I already pooped a few minutes ago. I'm just looking for some batteries I thought were in here."

Mom didn't push at the door again or ask me to close the cupboard. She said, "Well, that's good," and she left. The memories of my fright and subsequent relief remain vivid more than fifty years after the fact, as does my thankfulness for the providential design of that bathroom.

Mom's nature was the perfect counterbalance to mostly dry and unemotional Dad. She was warm and had a wide range of interests—current affairs, classical music, literature, and also sports. And she was always unabashedly bending the ears of strangers. Often, she'd embarrass me.

"Oh, my other son has a school ring that looks a lot like yours," she'd pipe to a young fellow in the checkout line at the A & P grocery. "It's from Jesuit High School. We sent him there because his dad went to a very good Jesuit school in St. Louis, our hometown. Have you ever been to St. Louis? Have you ever been to their zoo? It's really one of the best zoos in the country, and you don't have to pay. Everyone gets in free. Don't you think that's a nice way to do a zoo?"

But overall, Mom was a great communicator and soulmate. It was she who explained the birds and bees to me. We would often talk late in the evening, she in her favorite spot on the couch and me in a padded rocker, and one night when I was perhaps twelve, she launched right in.

"I remember you telling me about that blonde girl we saw at the fish fry last week," she said. "You told me you thought she was pretty. And it won't be that long before you'll probably start seeing some girls at dances or parties, so I think you're old enough to learn about how it really is between men and women physically."

Many parents never feel up to this conversation, to their kids' ultimate disadvantage, so great credit to Mom for this. I was well into messing with her lingerie by this time, and my interest in the girl at the fish fry was likely a mix between traditional attraction and envy of her pretty hair and cute clothes. But I was all in for the discussion. I knew I needed to know these things, and with Mom, I was comfortable learning about them.

"And that's how it all works," she said after maybe forty-five minutes, "and your knowing it is important as you get older. You are going to have physical urges, and when you understand, it's easier to stay out of any trouble. These aren't things you should feel guilty about—and wait! I think I forgot to tell you about something boys have. They're called 'wet dreams'..."

Mom was the parent who taught me tennis, a lifelong activity for me, and she reveled in the baseball lore of her hometown St. Louis Cardinals. And though not steeped in Texas sports tradition, through me she became an avid football fan. It started one fall day with me moaning piteously inside our living room.

"Honey, are you crying? Did you hurt yourself?"

"I'm OK," I called to her in the kitchen. "But the Cowboys just fumbled. Now they're gonna lose, and they'll probably miss the playoffs."

"Would it help if I watch a little with you?" she asked. "Maybe I can bring them some luck."

Soon she was watching every televised Cowboys game with me. Then she'd be counting, along with me, the hours until Thursday evening, when a half-hour of syndicated NFL highlights were aired by a local station. In this dark age, there were virtually no sports on television outside a few game broadcasts on weekends.

Then she lived a Cowboy fan's dream through her job. She had returned to nursing part-time when I became old enough to be alone at home, and by chance she wound up on the orthopedic ward of Baylor Hospital, where injured Cowboys were sent for surgery.

"Oh, I met Craig Morton today!" Mom would gush, referring to the Cowboys quarterback. "He's such a nice young man and very handsome, too. I helped him with a brace that was rubbing a raw spot on his leg, and he was very appreciative and called me 'Mrs. Brennan.' I told him all about you and how you love the Cowboys and want to be a sportswriter."

I bet she did. Several times.

Mom's enthusiastic side knew few bounds, particularly in the more manic periods of her later years, when she had moved to Cincinnati. In the fall of 1990, when I was thirty-eight and just done with covering the Reds' World Series season for *The Cincinnati Enquirer,* she made a lengthy debut on local sports talk radio. I experienced it, in a state of veiled horror, because I was in the studio as part of a writers' panel, trying to act the big-time professional sports dude.

"And now we'll go to Helen from Cincinnati," said Mike Bass, the show host. "Helen, how are you today?"

"I am doing just wonderfully, Mike"—yes, it was Mom— and I was lucky not to fall off my stool. I had told her of this radio appearance and knew she planned to listen, but not for an instant had I considered she might call in. Mom being Mom, I should have warned her not to. But now...what should I do? What could I do?

"I've only lived here a short time," Mom told Bass, also a local sportswriter, "but I have just become a huge Cincinnati sports fan. I love the Bengals, and I am just so thrilled about the Reds, and I love the job the media does. I can't wait to get the *Enquirer* every morning. Their writers are excellent, that Tim Sullivan and Jack Brennan."

I didn't respond. I didn't have to. Mom was going full blast with her new friend Bass.

"Baseball has always been my first love, Mike, especially the National League. I'm from St. Louis, and our whole family was always Cardinals fans. Did you ever hear of the Gashouse Gang, back in the '30s? Frankie Fritsch and Pepper Martin and Dizzy Dean? I was a teenager then, and they won the World Series twice. They were just so colorful!"

"Sure I've heard of 'em," said Bass. Mike was a big baseball fan himself and recognized Mom as an enthusiastic and informed caller. He let her roll on.

"And we loved the *Post-Dispatch* baseball stories," Mom said. "St. Louis was lucky to have such a great newspaper. But really, the *Enquirer* is a great paper, too. Jack Brennan and the other writers there are just so good."

Bass was still into this, finding it easy to poke Mom into more of her charming enthusiasm. Bad deal for me.

As it went beyond fifteen minutes, Bass began to discern a pattern. Whatever sports thing this Helen was waxing about, she would always come back to how great the *Enquirer* was and how much she enjoyed reading Jack Brennan.

"Jack, is this your mother?"

It was Bass, and he wasn't whispering or handing me a note. He was asking me directly, on the air.

"Yes, it is," I sheepishly confirmed. "Hi Mom, I didn't know you were going to call..."

"Oh Jackie, it's so good to hear your voice," she said. "I almost forgot you were there, I was having such fun talking to Mike. I hope I didn't embarrass you."

Bass cut in for me.

"Not in the slightest, Helen, and it has really been a pleasure talking to you today. I hope we hear from you again. Now all of Cincinnati knows you love your son very much."

Well, a portion of Cincinnati did, at least. Mike's show was on one of the city's smaller AM stations, so the damage was somewhat limited. And I never tried to scold Mom for it. She had meant so well.

## CHAPTER 4

# TINY CRACKS IN THE CLOSET DOOR

I was a tenth grader when I first risked wearing makeup outside my home. I recall doing it twice. They were electric experiences, frightening but very exciting. Pressure to *do something* had been building inside me for years. I did not want to be dramatically *caught* but I had a strong desire to be *seen* and to see any reaction it would cause.

First, I brought a lipstick to my all-boys' prep school and modeled it in the restroom. I had scouted out a likely way to have the restroom to myself, slipping out of class during a study hall. The school was small, and all other classes were in session. I adored the image in the mirror. Such a feminine boy. I wished I could be even more feminine. Totally feminine.

I allotted about ninety seconds for my thrill. Anything more would be madness, and ninety wasn't all that sane itself. Soon after, I had big pink stains on paper towels, which I stuck deep in the wastebasket under other trash, the way killers ditch bloody garments.

But no more than five minutes after I rejoined study hall, my classmate Tim Johnson remarked, devastatingly, "You look like you're wearing lipstick."

His tone was flat, drawing no one else's attention, and I tried to respond with nonchalance while slipping into panic mode. I muttered something about not knowing how that could be and how I guessed I needed to go look in a mirror. The restroom was still empty, thank goodness, and I scrubbed with soap almost to the point of drawing blood. I reentered study hall hoping it wouldn't be my last one as a normal guy.

And it wasn't. Tim paid no more attention, and how lucky was I that he had not made a big deal of it? Any number of others might have delighted in raising a crowd to inspect Brennan's suspiciously pink lips. I've often wondered if Tim had a low interest level because he simply could not have conceived something as titillating as the truth. Or—just possibly—did he suspect, or even *know,* and actually have a mind to protect me? I do recall Tim as among the smarter and more sensitive kids in the class.

Regardless, I had been spared the last thing any 1960s male teen could have wanted, exposure as a sissy in a den of sophomores at a Texas boys' school.

I duly promised myself not to tempt fate like that again, but I got over that soon enough. The urge to act out was not to be suppressed. A few weeks later, I lipsticked up before driving home from school. The way I had it figured, I'd bag the huge buzz of being feminized "in public" but would still be protected and essentially anonymous inside the car.

I did my lipstick in a secluded spot just beyond campus. I'd been in nonstop anticipation of this for days, and checking my pout in the rearview mirror was itself an unparalleled rush. I still vividly remember the fancy, girlish pattern on the gold lipstick tube. As I took off, I felt liberation as well as exhilaration.

My home was near the center of Dallas, about a thirty-minute drive from my western suburbs school. The first couple miles of my route were on two-lane roads with little traffic, and the thought arose, "What's the point in driving with lipstick on if nobody sees you?" But the main route to Dallas proper was the aforementioned Northwest Highway, with heavy traffic and frequent major intersections, and only minutes after being piqued at going unnoticed, I was wondering what the hell had made me think I'd like it if someone did notice.

Would they honk wildly and follow me? Beat me up? My world told me that things like that did happen. Didn't many consider it just a necessary form of maintenance to control societal vermin?

That's how I'd be regarded, and suddenly I felt terrified instead of titillated. It felt weird suddenly owning membership on the queer team, the one that always gets its ass kicked. Red lights appeared as deathtraps, setting up drivers on all sides with nothing to do for two minutes but people-watch.

*But isn't that what you wanted, pretty boy, to show yourself to the world?*

No, dammit, I've changed my mind. God help me get out of this. It was time to immediately switch back to the straight team, lest I be permanently consigned to that losing bunch of pansies. I turned off Northwest and into a gas station. All stations in 1960s Dallas had restroom entrances on their building exteriors, never locked, and they were usually around a corner from the activity of the pumps and service bays. Such a space was as good as could be had for a sissy in distress.

*But one false move out there, fag, and your ass will be slammed into lifelong shame as a homo. Even if you're not one.*

I could have parked right at the restroom door. But I was afraid to pull up that close, fearful of someone appearing suddenly from around a corner. Better to park a bit away, for a wider view of potential activity, and then boot-scoot it across the tarmac as soon as the coast cleared. I'd put one hand at my nose, like I maybe had a cold, to at least partially conceal those pansy lips.

But on my twenty-yard trek to the goal line, I was tripped up at the ten. The coast had been clear, but I'd forgotten something crucial. What if some guy was *already in the restroom?* I was stopped in my tracks, the worst insanity of all hitting me at this moment.

*Do* something*! You're out in the open with lipstick on! Go back to the car or into the goddam restroom!*

I rolled the dice and went for the room, which was blessedly unoccupied. But it had no paper towels and no soap. My toilet paper was disintegrating, and soaked in just cold water, it was barely affecting the pink tint. The stain was mocking in its imperviousness.

*You wanted to be a girl, so be one. You can't reverse it so quickly now. Wait until people see what a sissy you are.*

"Why couldn't you control yourself?" I thought. "You never should have done this, and you knew you never should have."

Back to the car, lips still pink. Back to Northwest Highway for a thrill ride that hopefully would not end before home. And it didn't. I had known that home would be empty, both parents at work, so plenty of soap and water later, I thought I looked OK again. The washcloth went deep in the trash, and as the sense of danger abated, so did any resolve to quit poking the bear.

I spared myself deep introspection about being such a strange fellow. I didn't ponder whether the urge to dress was more than I could resist or just stronger than I cared to resist. It was enough that it was compelling, a huge kick, and I was matter of fact about the continuing need to hide it from every other soul on earth.

# THE CD LIFE: LIPSTICK

Some say cross-dressing is just 10 percent paint and 90 percent attitude, and I applaud that ideal. But on days when 90 percent seems an impossibly high bar, I'm glad I've got lipstick.

Lipstick is powerful. Lipstick can sissify you more, in less time, than anything else in your makeup bag. It can make a plain male face look girly in thirty seconds flat. It's no mystery to me why the imprint of rouged lips is an icon of female sexiness in our culture.

Lipstick is easy to use. Just exercise a measure of precision for the sharp demarcation you want between your lip line and made-up skin, and you've pulled a sexy stunner for way less trouble than eyeliner or false nails. Lipstick is the cosmetic to set aside until you're done with more tedious parts of your preparation. It's a crowning glory. A reward for your hard work and a dramatic difference-maker as you complete your look.

Though lipstick offers countless pretty colors, my hobby of collecting photos leads me to full-blown reds or bold berrys. They define the mouth so much better than lighter colors. Don't get me wrong, pastel pinks can look super in the mirror, a real statement of soft sissy femininity. But pinks often get lost in a photo.

I once was excited to buy a dramatic teal shade, in an extra-shiny metallic formulation. But the more I looked in the mirror, the more it just looked weird, like a she-alien on *Star Trek*. Bottom line, teal is a hugely pretty color for nails, clothes, eyes, and shoes, but it's just too damn green for lips, unless you're the hot young magazine ad model who induced me to buy it.

Lip glosses are winners, too, whether clear or tinted. The shiny sexiness they impart is often a no-brainer for a hot night at the bar. But I prefer them applied over a good strong coat of traditional lipstick. The color is deeper that way, and often the gloss can add just the right change in hue to a lipstick color that's looking a little tired.

Great lipstick means so much to me, I once got concerned about it during a TV ad for—of all things—Ore Ida. The product was frozen potatoes and veggies, to be microwaved with an egg for a "hot scramble breakfast in no time." But as I watched a pretty young lady point a forkful toward her mouth, my thoughts quickly veered from the scramble's appetite appeal.

"What kind of damage will that do to her lipstick?" I asked, almost out loud. "It looks so perfect and freshly applied! If she's dashing right out for work, it might not look as cute as she'd like!"

I know, it was just an ad, and they wanted the lipstick on her in the shot. It reminded me of the women in mattress ads who wake up not only refreshed, but with their makeup salon-perfect. Even so, the Ore Ida ad left me making a mental note about lipstick:

Apply after breakfast, not before.

CHAPTER 5

# BRIEFLY A "NORMAL" GUY

As a high schooler, I had a hard time breaking into the dating game.

"I guess so," you're saying, "given you wanting to wear garters under your jeans and all that."

But I didn't spend every minute thinking about cross-dressing. I wanted to interact with girls in a very conventional way. Trouble was, I hardly knew any, much less had confidence with even one.

I largely blamed my school situation. Cistercian Preparatory School (CPS), an all-male Catholic institution, had been brand new when I was enrolled as a fifth grader. It was a project of Hungarian monks, members of the Cistercian order, who had formed a Greater Dallas community after fleeing Communism in their native land. My sister became enamored with these monks after studying under them at the Catholic-run University of Dallas, and when she heard of their plans for a boys' prep school, she convinced our parents to enroll me.

CPS launched with just two classes, a fourth grade and my fifth. To reach their vision of nine grades, fourth through twelfth, the monks planned to add a new fourth grade every year while the older classes moved up. For me and my fellow start-up fifth graders, this would offer the monstrous perk of eight straight years as the oldest class on campus. We were a tight group—numbering only thirty at the start and destined to fall below twenty in high school— and the monks were proud to proclaim us their "Pioneer Class." We came quickly to feel that we ran the place.

But Cistercian's embryonic status proved a drawback when I hit the crucial dating years, as there was no infrastructure for dances or other activities with girls' or coed schools. Most of my classmates seemed not to need such help, having connections from their neighborhoods or their own former elementary schools. But I lived in a different part of town than almost all my classmates—most were from wealthier backgrounds—and I found myself no longer a part of the social scene at my old coed parish school, St. Thomas Aquinas.

By the spring of my junior year, my loser status regarding girls was growing apparent to all and was on my mind every day. Classmates were going to dances and parties, some even bragging about sexual exploits. I coped for a while by latching more tightly to a good neighborhood friend two years younger than me, but it wasn't long until he began drifting toward his own school's party scene, leaving me hurting for a buddy to hang with on weekends. I knew I needed to change something to avoid a life as a lonely sports nerd, and getting cool with girls was going to be hard enough without letting cross-dressing get in the way. So even though I knew I was not fundamentally changed from that tiny kid who had longed to wear puffed sleeves, I managed to largely bury CD thoughts for the sake of development down the "normal" path. It was not so much a conscious decision, I think, as instinctive coping.

In September of my senior year, I was invited to a boy-girl party at the home of the only other kid from St. Thomas who had also switched to Cistercian. Tom Martin lived only a couple blocks from St. Thomas and had stayed in contact with many of our former classmates, becoming part of the mix as boys and girls came to discover one another.

Tom and I had always been tolerably friendly pals—we had even paired up as sophomores for Dallas Cowboys season tickets—but we were never among each other's closest buddies. So I knew I would come into Tom's party as a solo new guy. Some kids I wouldn't know at all, and others I would have barely seen since fourth grade. My invite, I sensed, came mostly from living nearby and from our parents having come to know each other through car-pooling us to CPS. I theorized it was perhaps not so much

Tom's idea as that of his very thoughtful mother. Regardless, I couldn't afford to pass on any chance to learn how to get on with girls.

But this opportunity proved out of my league. Unlike a boy-girl function at a school, where adults would at least somewhat direct the mingling—and where one could likely find a way to briefly disappear if need be—Tom's party was an intimate affair. Perhaps fifteen teens were gathered in the relatively tight space of the Martins' family room. Tom's parents were there but mostly out of sight. Everyone but me seemed to know each other well and be comfortably in the mix. I gravitated to a spot near the record player, feigning avid interest in the info on the album covers. I knew it was transparently pathetic.

During the party's later stages, to my considerable surprise, a girl from my old St. Thomas class suggested we dance. I had not particularly liked this girl as a fourth grader, but heck, I hadn't much liked any girls in fourth grade. She was quite attractive to me now, and very confident in her approach. We slow-danced arm in arm, but my nervousness left me with all the rhythm of a mannequin, and I could not think of one thing to say that I perceived she'd find interesting. I felt like a charity case, getting my one dance for the evening, and I was relieved when the party ended.

I had to just keep trying, so shortly after Thanksgiving, I forced myself to sign up for a weekend retreat for Catholic teens at the University of Dallas. "The Happening" was run by college-age progressives who aimed to show high schoolers that staying involved with the church could be cool. We would spend two nights on campus, engaging in adult-style discussions and guitar Masses and making new friends.

I didn't care about any of it except the new friends part. I had no path to a good life until I could break out of my shell. How wonderful and exciting it would be to find an attractive girl who actually seemed interested in *me*. I knew The Happening would force me into a sink-or-swim setting in mixed company, and that if I drowned again, like at Martin's party, it would be no worse than staying safely on shore with the latest copy of *Sports Illustrated*. I donned a windbreaker I thought was pretty cool—it showcased the Dallas Chaparrals of the American Basketball Association. I hoped it would at least lend me some confidence in my appearance.

And it was there that I met Valerie Kay Pilot.

I had resolved before arrival that for a change, I wouldn't let myself be paralyzed by fear of a faux pas. No hiding in the corner looking at album covers. Any screw-ups I made would be from trying too hard, not the reverse. It was on me to initiate contact with some girls, and it took all of five minutes at the opening reception to spot Valerie across the room. She was cute, with long brown hair, and she seemed approachable, engaged with some other kids in a lively way but apparently not part of a clique. I joined the group, sitting as close to her as I could manage without being obvious, and I aimed some conversation in her direction.

It was purely the small talk of seventeen-year-olds, school and related activities, but she seemed to enjoy it well enough. I learned she had grown up in Waco, one hundred miles south of Dallas, before moving as a high school junior to suburban Richardson, just north of Dallas proper. She attended the huge public Richardson High School, and her family lived in an apartment, factors that seemed racy and attractive to a prep school boy from a quiet neighborhood of single-family homes. But Val's parents were more sober and dutiful Catholics than my own folks, and they were anxious to leave the apartment at their first good opportunity to buy a Dallas home. Val had signed up for The Happening at the suggestion of a cousin who was among the event leaders.

She went by just Val, and my sole goal the rest of the weekend was staying in her orbit. Providentially, when the full attendance was divided into five groups of about twelve each, we were in the same cell. A leader arranged us in a circle, directing each kid to state his or her name and offer a brief introduction, and it was here that I scored a much-needed point.

"So who can go around the circle now and name every one of your fellow group members?" the leader asked after the intros.

Nervous laughter ensued, as if this were clearly beyond anyone's capability. But I was good at this kind of quick memorization, and I had focused on these names and faces, figuring that knowledge of my group environment could aid in avoiding some kind of massively embarrassing fuckup. So I volunteered to try, and I nailed every one. I even had the presence of mind to save Val's name for last, for my dramatic finish.

"Do you make straight As at your school?" Val said. "That's so neat that you could do that."

Neat? I picked up on that word. It was a bit out of style in 1969 teen jargon, and it had a most innocent quality. Kids bent on being perceived as hip might have said "wild" or "far out," had they commented at all. Val was showing me an unaffected quality that reinforced my confidence that I could just be myself with her.

I hit the sack in our dorm feeling good and looking forward to Saturday morning. But upon emerging from the restroom after my morning routine, I suddenly felt like returning to the john—to either puke, pound a metal stall door, or just cry. A new guy had been moved into our group, and he was breakfasting in the spot I had excitedly envisioned for myself, right next to Val. She didn't appear to even notice I had entered the room. She was all doe-eyed with this interloper.

"Oh, you should go there sometime," I heard him tell her. "It's a really cool party place."

*Oh, and I guess you just might be taking her there next weekend. Right, asshole?*

My state of mind at that moment can be best articulated with words repeatedly sung by Buck Owens and Roy Clark on *Hee-Haw*:

> *Gloom, despair, and agony on me.*
> *Deep dark depression; excessive misery.*
> *If it weren't for bad luck I'd have no luck at all.*
> *Gloom, despair, and agony on me.*

The interloper—we'll call him Jim Green—was taller than me. He was better dressed, with a tan suede jacket that made my Chaparrals windbreaker seem like kids' stuff. Worst of all, he had a sickeningly attractive mop of unapologetically fire-red hair and an outgoing personality to match. He had been placed on Earth, quite obviously, for the purpose of stomping out my tendril of a connection with Val.

I spent the rest of the weekend eating his dust. He even took Val out to the parking lot to show her *his* car, a Mustang the same color as his goddam hair. I didn't try to show her my ride. It was my mom's Plymouth Fury sedan, a four-door box in insipid canary yellow.

But though I was Mr. Third Wheel as the weekend played out, Val at least remained passably friendly. When I found her with a Jim-free moment, I asked for and obtained her phone number. I knew I wouldn't be using it for two weeks—there was no doubt she and Jim would be an item this next weekend—but I was ready to play the long game.

When The Happening broke up Sunday afternoon, everyone was in kumbaya mode. Even Jim and I.

*Fuck you, bastard*, I thought as I hugged him and smiled.

Nine days later, on a Tuesday evening, I called Val.

I planned it for just after eight, and I had never been so nervous as when call time approached. From about 6:30 on I just lay on my bed and semi-dozed, unable to focus on anything else. Trying to ensure I wouldn't be tongue-tied when we spoke, I had prepared a written list of conversation stimulants:

"Well, what did you think of The Happening?" Pretty lame.

"So what's it really like at a huge school like Richardson?" Somewhat better.

"I remember you said you like Simon & Garfunkel. I really do, too. Do you have any of their albums?" Not bad, perhaps.

Off went my alarm. I had wanted to make sure I didn't doze off completely. It was five minutes to eight.

The phone rang three times, and then it must have been her father answering. He was happy to fetch her without grilling me.

"Hi Val, it's Jack Brennan from The Happening," I said, as brightly as I could. *And I think you're so pretty and sexy, I would just about die to have a date with you and transform my life from abysmal to awesome in a second.*

That's what I wanted to say, but instead I just said I wanted to "check up and see how you're doing" and thanked her for giving me her number.

"Well, hey, thanks for calling," she said. "I was just finishing some homework, but I can do it later. How are *you* doing?"

*Me.* She wanted to know what was up with *me*, and I suspected right away that the Jim Green date had fallen short of spectacular. Otherwise her tone would have been different. This beautiful girl actually did *not* think I was a creep for calling, and it turned out I didn't need those notes I had worked up. Val was easy to talk to.

"So, hey, what would you think about getting together this Friday?" I asked. "Maybe we could go to a movie and then get something to eat."

"I've got to check with my parents," she said, "but I think it should be fine. I'd like to."

I wasn't on cloud nine just yet. I remained very unsure of myself. But for the first time, I had gotten myself a date with a pretty girl who was at least mildly interested in me.

My nerves returned in full force on Friday when I got back in the Fury and drove to Richardson. I got there way early and just sat in the car in a shopping center for a half hour. But she looked super great when I picked her up, and hot damn, she snuggled up right next to me on the Fury's bench seat, the way girls did with their guys in those days.

We went to see *Butch Cassidy and the Sundance Kid*, an excellent first-date movie, happy and wholesome but somewhat hip. But I didn't care if it was a documentary on needlework as long as Val seemed to be enjoying it. I was so excited just to be with her, tingles of desire and delight ran up my spine when she just slightly leaned her head back on my arm as we sat in the theater. Who says your elbow can't be an erotic zone?

We stopped by a Big Boy hamburger restaurant afterward, and though she chose not to eat—maybe she was nervous, too—the conversation was still smooth. I had been a fry cook at this eatery for a brief stint, a fairly interesting summer job for a high school kid, so I could wax on a little about that. The booths had those old-school individual jukeboxes, and I ponied up a quarter for "The Boxer," a new Simon & Garfunkel tune we both had come to like.

I didn't try to kiss Val when we got back to her home. I think she expected me to, maybe wanted me to, but my confidence level was still too low. But she agreed to a second date, and I kissed her on that one, and I kept on asking her out. She said in mid-January that it might be good for us to take a little break, but I talked her out of it, and on February 18 she accepted my class ring. We kissed like crazy in her living room—her parents were cool enough to not get in the way—and when we were done, I could have buzzed the twelve miles back to my house without the Fury.

And what of the bastard Jim Green? Not long into our courtship, I learned from Val that she indeed had been less than thrilled with their date. His miscues had included a failed bid to impress her with fast driving, and he also had been too physically aggressive. She said that as she looked back, she was glad I *hadn't* tried to kiss her that first night.

It couldn't really have been more perfect, this dead of winter in 1970. But by late spring, my urge to dress would end its hibernation, and I would be hiding it again.

CHAPTER 6

# BACK IN THE GAME

As Valerie and I tripped through the end of winter and into spring of our senior year, we became sexually active. She had no clue of my experience with lipstick and garter belts.

But, of course, it was unthinkable that she could ever know. As of spring 1970, only the *really queer* queers, in places like New York or San Francisco, were coming out. It would be still another four years until homosexuality was removed from classification as a "disorder" by the American Psychiatric Association. As for transgenderism, it wasn't until spring of 2019 that the World Health Organization stopped categorizing it as a disorder or mental illness.

And what would have been the point of trying to tell Val anyway? I hadn't been doing any dressing or even thinking about it much for more than a year. Life was truly magical for me. I had a girl I really clicked with, I truly did love her so, and I knew she loved me. I was just so proud and delighted to finally be a part of my high school social set with her at my side. I thought dressing was quite possibly just a part of my past.

Until it wasn't. Once it became clear that Valerie and I were truly in love—so tight that by midsummer of '70 we would pledge to marry after college—my urges resurfaced. Finding a spark with a conventional relationship had unexpectedly proven to be a trigger. With Valerie in my life, my core goals of dating, eventual marriage, and a family were now unfolding. With that security, I found my libido asking why dressing—in secret, of course—could not be accommodated once again.

So was it devils or angels who sparked my return to dressing by providing an impossibly rare opportunity? Take your pick, but in April 1970 I would be requested to strut my girl stuff *on a stage.* Our drama teacher at Cistercian had chosen a slapstick nineteenth-century melodrama for our spring production, and all the roles—including the damsels in distress— would be played by us boys.

A couple guys flatly refused female parts. I, of course, was delighted to comply, as my cover couldn't have been more secure. It was a school deal, there were others also willing to play girls' roles, and the whole idea was generally accepted as a hoot. Less than three months after my successful pursuit of Val, I was reveling in my role as "Angela Angleworm," and to an extent no one could be allowed to know.

We "girls" had been encouraged to wear makeup, and I went hog wild with the mascara. After we were all presumably ready, I found time to head back to the boys' room to enjoy putting on a couple extra coats. Just following instructions, right? I didn't want to look just like a boy in a dress in a farcical comedy. I wanted to look like a real girl—as close to it as possible, anyway. After the performance, I lingered in my costume for as long as I thought I could get away with it. It was mind-blowing—profoundly unprecedented—to be talking and laughing with others while "en femme" (the French phrase CDs favor to describe being fully dressed) and to have neither adults nor kids acting like I was a sickening homo.

Valerie didn't suspect a thing, and neither did anyone else, I thought. But weeks later, as our graduation activities proceeded, I was shaken regarding the latter assumption.

We were passing around our newly arrived school yearbooks, collecting written messages from each other for posterity. It was an intimate and personal session by comparison with the high school norm, since there were only seventeen of us by this point and we had mostly been together for eight years.

But one classmate's message in my book made me gulp.

"Jackie," he had written, using a nickname I had long since strived to drop, "you always acted like it, but your peak came when you played a girl in the school play."

"Very funny," I told him, heart racing.

"Hey, I just call 'em as I see 'em," came the reply.

Then we both laughed and moved on. I was not being confronted or challenged on this, thank God.

The dual tracks of conventional sexual activity and CD fantasies went forward for me. Sex with Valerie was great, but there were just so many CD triggers—makeup ads, supermarket fashion magazines, babes in heels on TV. As for the sex life, aside from rare occasions when one of our homes was available, Val and I got in each other's pants in the back seats of our family cars.

"Parking" was the teenage term for it, and our favorite spot was an unlighted field adjoining the Moody Coliseum on the SMU campus. It was used for basketball game parking and very little else. (It became, I've been told, part of the site for George W. Bush's Presidential Library.) Weekends back then with no basketball would find the field hosting numerous vehicles filled with young folks seeking a different kind of balling. Getting just the right spot could be tricky; it was rather like trolling for a place at a drive-in movie when you'd arrived late and the lights were already killed. Once sited, we had to be aware of occasional cruising cops, but they usually looked the other way for couples being reasonably discreet.

Also popular with us, albeit only briefly, was a secluded parking lot behind a big Protestant church in North Dallas, closer to Val's home. We seemed to be its only late-night customers, and after a couple of visits, we felt safe completely disrobing. But on about our fourth trip, ecstasy vanished in a maelstrom of sound and fury. Younger boys—five or six of them, maybe age twelve or thirteen—had discovered our hideaway and were beating on the car while screaming their damn heads off.

I scrambled into the driver's seat, still naked. My anger was such that I desperately wanted to acquaint at least one of them with mortal fear by doing a very close brush-by with the car. Thankfully, they decamped swiftly enough to deny me any chance. I seethed about the incident for weeks.

Those kids had nailed us big time. But we returned to SMU for subsequent trysts, and sex still ran hot until August, when our world seemed suddenly to be crashing down.

Knowing full well that our efforts with condoms and vagicides had been inconsistent, we became terrified when Valerie's somewhat predictable menstrual cycle failed to kick in. Our fear reached a crisis point on a Saturday night, as we failed miserably to enjoy a dinner out.

"How late do you think you are?" I asked.

"How can I know exactly?" said she. "It's not like I write 'em down. My last period was in early July but I don't know the dates. It just seems like I should have had another one by now."

"Can you remember being this late before but having it come after not much longer?"

"I don't know, Jack. I really just don't know."

She was crying at this point. I tried to comfort her, unsuccessfully.

Sunday came and went. Then Monday. Then Tuesday. They were the most awfully worried days I'd ever experienced. It was better to not be with Val all the time, as I could divert myself for brief periods alone. But the dark cloud would reliably return, followed by a hammer to the gut. I envisioned nothing short of a two-family calamity. It was only four weeks before our planned departures for college, and we weren't even headed for the same school. Shit, there wouldn't be any college for either of us in 1970–71 if her period didn't kick in, and who knew if there would be college at all? We were looking at being parents by May. What kind of godforsaken job might I have had to accept by that point?

"Jack, it's OK!"

It was eight on Wednesday morning. I was at home. Val was calling from Richardson.

"I started! We're OK!"

I was talking on the only phone in our house, right in the middle of everything, at the head of a hallway connecting the living room and bedrooms. Mom was in the living room. Thankfully the phone cord would extend into my bedroom, because I was audibly gasping with relief.

"I'll be there in twenty minutes," I finally said to Val.

"I'm going to Val's," I told Mom.

"A little early, isn't it?"

"It's just a thing not worth explaining now, but everything's fine," I said.

I didn't wait to see if Mom had a response. I had carte blanche to use her car unless she told me otherwise, and I sped north on Central Expressway to Richardson. I hung around all day, and we celebrated that evening at a place offering Maine lobster dinners for $4.95.

"Pretty fancy for a weeknight," Val's dad observed.

The lobster was excellent. I was much into seeking out new cuisines after a very conventional childhood diet. But despite our dodging of snake eyes in a six-month crapshoot with reproductive biology, Valerie and I had serious matters to discuss.

"Mother almost caught me crying the other night," Val said. "I told her it was allergies. I took some Benadryl to help convince her. I don't know what I'd have told her if she had really caught on."

"I had very bad dreams last night," I said. "There was this room with our parents and some kind of judge-type guy, and I think our college plans were getting cancelled. It was one of those dreams you have when you're still dozing but you know it's time to get up. I was only up for like 15 minutes when you called. Oh, it was so sweet when you called!"

I went around the table and hugged her. Kissed her, too, of course. Nobody in the place seemed to mind.

"It was the middle of the night when I noticed," Val said. "I thanked God and Saint Theresa. I wanted to call you right away."

"Glad you didn't. What would I have said to Mom and Dad?"

"But I am not going to ever face this ever again," she said. "I don't care if we don't make love again until we're married."

But I knew she did care about that.

"You know the thing to do," I said. "We need to get you birth-control pills. We were so stupid not to have done it already. You're eighteen, nobody has to know. Didn't Diane say she'd help you? Go with you to Planned Parenthood?"

Diane, Val's sister-in-law, was a late-twenties cool adult. She and Val were close.

"I always worried worry about Mother or Daddy or Tami finding the pills," Val said. Tami was her twelve-year-old sister. "Or that they'd make me throw up or something and I'd have to explain that."

"It's pregnancy that makes you throw up," I said, "not the pills. Isn't that right? Look, I'm not trying to make you do anything. But would you at least just talk to Diane?"

She did, and five days later we were back in business. But a dreadful thing was still on our near horizon, as bad as could be without a death in the family or us having done something horribly wrong (like getting pregnant). The remaining days of August were peeling away with astonishing speed, bringing the dates when we'd head for college—separately.

I was bound two hundred miles south to the sprawling University of Texas in Austin, the best school at a middle-class price for the pursuit of the journalism degree that I hoped would land me a career around sports. But Val's folks, Alan and Theo, didn't feel she was ready for UT. Or maybe it was they who weren't quite ready. Regardless, Val would commence matriculation at East Texas State University, a much smaller school just sixty miles northeast of Dallas. It was rather a "shit-kicker" school to an urbane Dallasite like myself, with rural culture ruling the place.

I left town first, driven to Austin by Mom and Dad on the morning after an evening when Val and I had shed buckets of tears. We hadn't needed to pledge to be true to each other. That was 100 percent presumed. We just knew we were going to miss each other terribly. We'd been fully together for six months, and that was possibly the worst amount of time for this to now be happening. We were already at the point of hardly thinking about our old lives without each other, yet every day was still so new and exciting.

The social aspects of our freshman college experiences were largely just lost to us. We had been encouraged by our folks to date others at least a little, as they couldn't help fear we had bonded too quickly and tightly. But neither of us did more than a token.

I needed a date for a couple of major parties at Delta Sigma Phi, the fraternity where I had pledged. As a left-wing adult, I find it less mortifying to come out as a CD on these pages than to admit having been a social fraternity member. But I had gone through rush because my well-meaning dad strongly encouraged me that a small-group identity could help me at such a large university.

I found a nice date for both big parties: a former grade-school classmate I had happened upon in a lecture class. Tracy D. was a sharp and pretty girl, and I think she really liked me, too. But I had to tell her up front about Val, and I felt bad about not being fully into our dates. I just had no interest in being with any other girl, however vibrant and attractive.

This was more than twenty years before wide use of cell phones, and landline long-distance calls were pricey. So Val and I wrote each other almost daily. But that was thin gruel for our spirits, and by the end of September we were both scheming to come home at least every other weekend. I had no car, so I became an avid reader of campus bulletin boards, where students who made regular trips to Dallas and other major cities would advertise for riders to share gas costs.

Valerie had no trouble finding rides from her relatively close location, and we both resisted our parents' entreaties to spend more weekends on campus. I eventually found a guy who went to Dallas almost every weekend, but I had to fit his schedules for departure and Sunday return, sometimes to the detriment of schoolwork. The travel itself stunk, as I was crammed for nearly four hours each way into the tiny back seat of a two-door Chevelle SS coupe, my knees almost in my face.

The guy had a close buddy who always got the bucket passenger seat in front, and though sometimes I could stretch out a little across the back seat, often that was precluded by another paying rider sharing it with me. The guys in front favored a head-pounding stereo level, and for years I could not hear Santana's "Oye Como Va" without flashbacks of these trips.

It was all a price worth paying, though, especially on those late Friday afternoons bright with the promise of forty-eight hours with my lover. We'd go out Friday night, do something early Saturday, and then go out Saturday night.

But the piece of Sunday we'd have was bittersweet to the max. We couldn't get together early enough to avoid the shadow of my roughly 3:00 p.m. return to Austin. We'd cry as my ride arrived, causing me the need to mop up before heading to the car. The trip back was long and dreary, bifurcated by a "halfway there" pass through Val's hometown of Waco, where the city's only tall building, the twenty-two-story Amicable Insurance tower, stood out starkly in the bleak night. It suggested to me the normal lives that would be pursued in downtown on the morrow, but such untroubled routine would not be for me. My UT dorm room, which I shared with a really goofy fellow, seemed unwelcoming. And Monday morning meant a return to class with some assignments likely done to less than perfection.

UT was a cool school—I was proud to be a student there—but May 20, 1971, could not have come soon enough for me. Freshman year was over, and it was summer again, when Val and I would be together in Dallas. Unalloyed joy never seemed to last, however, because by late June we were obsessively awaiting the mail each day. Nothing less than lives worth living was hanging in the balance, because Val's parents had permitted her to apply to UT.

"Val, here's a letter for you," her mom said one July day. Though she surely knew the official-looking envelope from Austin contained either wildly wonderful or totally crushing news, she handed it to Val as if it were a mailer from Walgreens and went to her sewing room. Val and I were left unaccompanied in the living room.

We held hands for a few moments. We had rated her chances as a toss-up, because at that time UT was said to approve about 50 percent of transfer applications. We lingered and stared. As long as the envelope remained sealed, the Schrödinger's cat of acceptance remained potentially alive inside.

"Open it," I finally told her.

"I can't," she said. "You open it."

I proceeded very carefully.

"Hurry up!" she pleaded.

But who knew the rules on this? Maybe if you got accepted you had to sign something and send it back, and maybe if you tore the letter, the deal was off. Some neater but less promising kid on the next block would wind up copping the spot instead. I was literally that scared of somehow fucking up the most important outcome in my life.

It was a handsome letter, embossed with the school logo, and thank God, it didn't beat around the bush:

"Congratulations, Valerie," I read aloud with glee. "Your application to enter the University as a Fall 1971 sophomore student has been accepted."

She was so proud. She had never been a top student in report-card reckonings, but her East Texas State marks were better than anything she'd produced in high school. And I was just so pumped. Suddenly I wanted the summer to end and September in Austin to be upon us. We hollered to Val's mom and younger sister, and her mom called her dad at work, and when she was done, I called my house. Family plans for Val's big move began immediately.

I was already set for sophomore housing, assigned a room in the ramshackle Delta Sigma Phi house. (We weren't a wealthy group as Greeks went, if that makes me seem a bit less frat boy.) Val would be in the Andrews Hall girls' dorm on campus. Still carless, we saved our summer job money to buy two brand-new Schwinn Varsity ten-speed bikes. They felt like Corvettes to us. Her girls' model was a beautiful Creamsicle orange, and I envied it, because my boys' version had been available only in a dull brown. But if she had been forced to settle for a brown one as well, perhaps that would have been better, as her bike was stolen just a week after our arrival. She was devastated at the way the cruel world had treated her, and I felt angry and powerless to help.

Nothing, however, could put a lasting damper on our newfound experience. Val was able to obtain a serviceable, if lesser, bike, and now we were living almost as two adults, in a wonderland of possible new activities. I was most delighted just to finally have a pretty girlfriend to strut around the fraternity house. As a freshman, it had been a deathly drag to tell the few who cared to listen about my cool girl back home while others were partying it up.

The culture of the times still sternly frowned on any form of cohabitation among college kids, and the university tried hard to enforce it on campus. Val had overnighted in my dorm room one time when we were freshmen— the only time she made it down to my campus for a weekend—and the experience had not been much fun, fraught with fears of getting caught. But the frat house was not encumbered by any Puritan policies, so Val spent numerous nights with me, especially after I switched to a third-floor room with a private outside entrance off an easy-to-climb fire escape.

But during that first fall together, even before I switched to the more private room, I was in possession of a bra.

## CHAPTER 7

# HONESTY NEVER STOOD A CHANCE

I struggle to recall how I obtained the bra, as I was many years from being brave enough to purchase lingerie. I could have stolen it from my mom or Valerie, but I remember it as an ample bra with big cups, larger than either of them would have worn. Could it have been Val's sister-in-law Diane's? She was more ample-bosomed, but I can't see how I'd have possessed one of hers.

Whatever its provenance, the bra was with me in my frat house room this fall of 1971. On the night I took it from its hiding place, I started by examining it just for its own sexiness. The cups were embroidered with flowers. Then came a head rush, and a rush to lock my door. I would put it on. I had to put it on.

Getting it fastened was difficult. I had to don it backwards at first, so I could see the hooks. But after a couple minutes, it was on, and I was stuffing it with socks. When I buttoned an Oxford dress shirt over it, my new girlish figure took shape.

Oh, yeah.

I spoke it aloud.

Visually, it was electrifying. How many sets of sexy breasts had I ogled in the past ten years while wishing I could have a pair myself? Palpably, it was arresting. I couldn't ignore the binding feel around my chest. Emotionally, it was vindicating. I needed these feelings.

I needed to sometimes have tits, dammit. That's what I called them to myself, and that's what I've most often called them in all my years of dressing. Whatever one calls them, the ones I created with gym socks and my bra were emotionally explosive for me. What environment could have been more fraught with potential peril for this exercise than a house full of Texas frat boys? And my locked door did not guarantee full security. A fastened and stuffed bra under a buttoned shirt is not subject to instant removal, and what if a frat brother started knocking and asking why I was locked in? Worse yet, what if a gang of pledges, having secured the house manager's master key, was bent on the time-honored prank of abducting a member and dumping him fully clothed into a nearby sorority swimming pool? Such unruliness was not rare in this residence and could develop with lightning speed.

It was barely two minutes before I deemed my action a madman's caper and struggled out of my halter. I felt relieved, but also profoundly unsatisfied. More than I realized, I think, I was angry and intensely frustrated over my very nature being seen by my world as so wrong. The people who mattered most in my life—Valerie, close friends, even family—could, in a flash, be led to turn away from me, or even turn on me. My imagination ran wild with my fears. They'd all be thinking I had screwed-up parents, an abusive uncle, a personality disorder, a hormone problem, or all of the above. They'd be talking all the time about what a scream and also how sad it was that Jack Brennan is a little sissy.

But it wasn't as if these feelings were anything new. The way forward for me had always been, and continued to be, to just cover it up and play straight. I didn't for one second consider trying to proudly live my true self, because in my slice of Texas, the extreme limit for anything like that was owning up to eating an occasional pork chop instead of beef. There was nothing to do but maintain my inner conviction that whatever humiliation society might potentially heap on me, I was not as perverted as people would think.

Playing straight wasn't even really "playing" for me, not the large majority of the time. Unlike the experiences of transsexuals I've read, to just be a guy among guys came as naturally as breathing to me. I could feel that naturally yet still wish that I could trade clothes and bodies with a blonde blind date I once had as a freshman at a Texas football game. She was pretty, with long blonde hair, and wore a really cute orange jumper. I wasn't great date for her, for just as with Tracy D., I didn't want to be dating anyone but Val. But I took keen interest in my date's looks and imagined looking and dressing like that and going to a game with a guy.

But it was that first sophomore semester, when I messed with the bra, that marked a point from which my urge to dress would never be far from mind.

College life afforded almost no chances for safe and fun activity, however, so it all stayed 98 percent in my head until a landmark summer night in 1973, prior to my final semester at UT. It was my last summer as a student before entering adulthood. Our wedding was planned for December 29, right after I would graduate. (Val and I had not become engaged at any specific time, and there was never a formal "popping of the question." It had just organically come to be for two lovers who had concurred back in high school that we would marry upon my graduation.)

But the wedding was not on my mind on this summer night, because I was messing with high heels for the first time. If I could have but one feminine item, I'd probably go with heels. Nothing feels more feminine than wearing them.

For this first try at heels, I had a pair of modest white sandals with heels of perhaps an inch and a half. I had bought them with much trepidation at a Kmart, where you could just take your size right off a shelf rather than dealing with a clerk. Not that I was sure of my size in women's shoes, but the biggest size on the shelf was a ten, so I had grabbed that and hoped for the best. To get through checkout with minimal notice, I had camouflaged the shoes by filling my basket with things a regular guy would buy, including paper towels, school supplies, a can of tennis balls, and—a brilliantly manly choice—two quarts of motor oil. Still, I was nervous as hell, but I managed to close the deal without incident.

Val and I both still lived with our parents during the summer, and things had worked out for me to test-drive my new footwear at her house. Her parents and her younger sister Tami were in Waco visiting family, and she was working a two-to-ten-p.m. shift at a nearby retail store. She had no access to a car because the family's second vehicle was in the shop, so it had been determined that I would take her to work and then hang at the Pilot home until it was time to pick her up. I don't remember whether I bought the heels that very afternoon or had brought them from a hiding place at my house.

When I put the heels on and stood up, the feeling made my head spin, exceeding any previous notion of what it might be like. I felt an almost literal jolt of electricity from my toes up through my groin. Gentle as their incline was, it made me instantly feel magnificently feminine. I knew that from this point forward, any earnest effort at dressing on my part would include a pair of heels.

I also did something else for the first time that night. With those heels on, I went to the refrigerator for a pack of smoked sausages. I took one out, and after a bit of wiggling and maneuvering, I managed to stick it up my ass. I was still a long way from having my first dildo—I would not have known how to obtain one—and this had been the closest thing to an erect penis that I could find at the grocery. It was my first time to act out a growing new reality, admitting to myself that when I was dressed, I was excited by the concept of taking womanhood all the way: being penetrated.

The actual process, however, was awkward and tinged with some measure of guilt. It wasn't nearly as purely exciting and fun as wearing the heels. The feeling was mostly just strange. Did I masturbate with the wiener still within? It seems in hindsight that I would have, but I carry no memory of that. The guilt aspect may have kept me from it. Regardless, I ended that first session by resolving I wouldn't be doing that anymore. I didn't feel terrible about myself, but it just seemed a bridge too far.

And I would hold to that resolution for a few years. But the bottom line in this summer of '73 was that, with my marriage fast approaching, I was back to cross-dressing occasionally, and I found its allure overpowering. I was able to reconcile those feelings with the emotion and energy of our wedding plans because it wasn't anything new for me to conceal my urges and activity. As soon as I was done wearing heels (and sausage) at Valerie's house, I clicked back into fiancé mode and proceeded to get her at work.

*You cad. Might it have ever crossed your mind that Valerie deserved to know something about this before the wedding?*

Of course it crossed my mind. I wasn't *that* big of a cad to not even mull it over. I had no doubt that among potential threats to our relationship, cross-dressing was a ten on a ten scale. But whatever consideration I might have given it, the idea of coming out before the wedding really never had a chance.

Deep as I knew our love to be, I feared it couldn't survive knowledge of my craving the sexual charge of such a despised practice. How could Valerie help but have second thoughts or, more likely, just call the whole thing off? And then what would we tell friends and relatives? No lies would be adequate, and declining all comment would be untenable.

Even if Val somehow still wanted me, she would have to tell somebody. Certainly her parents, and though they were great, loving people with a real love for me, this was a development almost no one would be prepared to face. They probably would withdraw their support for our union, coming to feel that the good of their daughter demanded it, and the process would be more ugly and painful than anything they'd experienced in their fifty years of life.

They'd never be able to look at me again. My parents still would, of course, but it would never be the same for me with them or with friends and relatives. The most palatable thing for everyone—and the best thing, most would agree—would be to treat me as a poor unfortunate with a serious behavioral disorder. Simply put, I'd be branded as a homo, and what did people actually do with homos in their families in 1970s Texas? They laid low and hid it as best they could, far as I could tell. I didn't personally know anyone out as gay, and if anybody I knew had such knowledge, they weren't sharing it with me. Maybe, since I was twenty-one with a college degree, I could move somewhere and start a new life, in the closet of course. I could still see the family sometimes.

Would I get any credit for fessing up prior to the wedding? Hell, no. I'd be derided as a sneaky fag who should have stayed in his little dresses and not deceived a great young woman into a relationship that clearly had no future. "How could he have done that to her?" people would ask. "How could he have led on their families like that and then blown the whole thing up?"

So I never came within a country mile of a prenuptial coming out. It seemed I'd be throwing my whole life in a shredder. I couldn't conceive of giving Valerie up—I simply wasn't going to—and the way to ensure our marriage would happen as planned was simply not to do a damn thing.

When the Big Question would arise in my mind, I'd manage to dismiss it and go on with life. When it rose the next time, I'd dismiss it again. I was not constantly torn up about it. The recurring thoughts were not so very different from the way the whole cross-dressing thing had been somehow manageable all along. I believed I could keep it secret. I was mostly having great fun during the weeks leading up to our wedding. Valerie and I were the toast of our families and our circle of friends.

My very large can of CD concerns was just going to get kicked down the road a bit farther.

# THE CD LIFE: HEELS

Difficult as wearing heels can be—and on many levels it's about the stupidest thing a sentient being could do—let's be careful what we'd wish for. Heels wouldn't be nearly as much fun if anybody could just throw on a pair and work 'em like they were sneakers.

When you're in heels, you are special. But you have to earn it. You are making a bold statement of your wild desire to be traditionally feminine and super sexy. You like the way heels limit your movement to mincing steps. You take girly pride in the skill required to maneuver in them. And of course, they make your legs and butt and boobs look great.

Heels are deemed a must by the entertainment industry for women who depend at least partially on their looks to make a buck. Valerie regularly watches Kelly Ripa's show on morning TV, and I've noticed that in addition to Kelly wearing very hot heels every single day, her female guests under a certain age almost always wear them, too.

But Kelly and company are usually just wiggling their pretty feet while comfortably seated. For a prize-winning performance from someone who couldn't sit, I nominate an attractive young woman whose husband was receiving a high school football coach of the year award at Paul Brown Stadium.

The Bengals annually conferred the honor as part of a preseason media luncheon. My duties at this event were not taxing, and I spent a lot of time stealing glances at the honoree's wife, who we'll call Ginger in this retellling. She was maybe thirty-two, great figure, in a great dress— and stunning heels.

Ginger and her husband were chatting with Bengals front-office personnel, all parties standing, while media members pursued interview opportunities with team president Mike Brown, head coach Marvin Lewis, and some of Lewis's assistants. These interviews always went on for the better part of an hour before lunch, and during this time I kept noticing Ginger standing on those spikes on a hard and rather slippery terrazzo floor.

Fifteen minutes...twenty-five...forty-five...how could she possibly keep doing it? Was she screaming behind that pretty smile, desperate for the call to lunch? Or was she just so much better than me in stilettos? I figured I'd be good for fifteen minutes max standing in those shoes, and then I'd have needed to be carried to my chair.

Probably Ginger's heels were high-end and relatively well-fitting. Surely they couldn't have been pinching her toes. You simply cannot wear heels that pinch your toes with your weight bearing down. It won't go away, you won't "get used to it," and you'll be crying for a bench after twenty yards.

And I trust Ginger was not plagued by a strap or buckle biting into her ankle. This is something a heel-wearer may notice only gradually, and they might think it doesn't really hurt that much. But gutting it out will leave you with a thin-but-deadly bright red gash that will torment you for quite some time. It might render you unable to wear other favorite shoes for a while, as these cuts are exceptionally slow to heal. If you find yourself in this fix, just carry your heels the way girls do when it's late at the prom if you can. I've always thought that was a great look, almost as sexy as wearing 'em.

A really good pair of heels is worth taking to a repair shop when the heel tip wears away and exposes a metal stud. It's awkward to enter such an old-fashioned male world with a couple pairs of heels, but it's worth it to get a whole new round of duty from a sexy pair that allows you to walk with confidence.

Even the most seemingly comfortable heels will bite you if you give them enough chance, however. I once marched in a gay pride parade wearing very conservative wedges, shoes I had felt I could walk in forever. But after an unexpectedly long route of several miles, my feet were so numb and sore that I worried about semipermanent damage.

Thankfully that wasn't the case. May we all go on working it confidently in our heels, just like the women on *Dancing with the Stars*. The steps those ladies execute in four-inch heels are enough to earn them an Emmy.

## CHAPTER 8

# BLUE EYESHADOW CAN BE A DRAG

The wedding went great, once we got past the part where Val nearly collapsed from nerves on her way to the altar.

The date for the Saturday afternoon affair was December 29, 1973. The site was the chapel of the Cistercian Abbey, just a stone's throw from the prep school. The guest list was about one hundred. The scene was not lavish, but it crackled with excitement, as Val and I were the first of our high-school crowd to marry.

Val had always felt scared to be the center of attention. She was also very thin, barely over one hundred pounds, and though the ceremony didn't start until three o'clock, she may not have eaten all day. She appeared both physically and emotionally unstable as her dad tried to lead her up the aisle; he clearly had all he could handle to forestall an early disaster. Alan Pilot leaned his face in close to Val, delivering whispered encouragement, and he held her erect with a strong arm around her waist, walking all the while at a slow but steady pace. Poor Valerie was trying so hard to be brave and smile, but so frozen was her expression, it was as if she feared the flick of an eyelash might bring her shattering in pieces to the floor.

Never in zillions of hours watching football had I rooted harder for a key player (Mr. Pilot) to advance the ball (Valerie) just fifteen more yards. It was all Mr. Pilot, really. He got his daughter safely into the end zone, so to speak, and handing her off to me at the altar, he looked at me as if to say, "It's on you now to get her through the rest of this."

Recalling it can make me both laugh and cry. The memory of Valerie's vulnerable sweetness is just so tender. But once we were set in front of the officiating cleric, she did fine. Vows, rings, Mass, the whole deal.

"When it was time to walk in, I just got a case of the shakes," Val told me after the ceremony. "The idea of being 'on display' in a tight dress in front of all those people…I just worried that I couldn't handle it."

*Wow, what a waste*, I would joke to myself at some point a bit later. *Let me wear the tight dress in front of a crowd.*

Those kinds of thoughts were never awfully far away.

"I couldn't have done it without Daddy," Val concluded. "He told me we were going to make it, and we did. I wanted to make it for him."

After officially becoming Mr. and Mrs. Brennan, we did cake and punch and photos in the school lunchroom, and shortly thereafter the festivities were concluded. But one key person had been missing through it all. My dad.

Thankfully, it wasn't because he was passed out drunk. Late Friday afternoon, barely twenty-four hours before the wedding, Mom had rushed him to Baylor Hospital, reporting him as dazed and disoriented.

"He kept asking about the mail," Mom said to me in a call from the hospital. "He couldn't grasp that I already showed it to him right after lunch."

Mom said she feared he'd suffered a stroke or a blunt trauma head injury, noting that several hours previously, he had slipped on a wet spot in the kitchen and fallen into a cabinet.

"It seemed like he shrugged that off," she said. "He was sitting and reading the paper afterward. But you can still see the knot on his forehead."

The doctors never figured out what it was. They agreed he was disoriented upon admission, but no stroke or blunt trauma effect was found, and by seven o'clock that evening he seemed fine again. He wouldn't be out in time for the wedding—he was to be under observation at least through Saturday night—but Mom said he was insisting that the festivities go on as planned.

And so things did, and then we brought a bit of the wedding to Dad, traipsing to his room in our nuptial finery. We had a nice visit, with Val and me quietly thankful that his incident had not been related to alcohol abuse, at least not directly.

Then we had a quick change of clothes, a wedding night dinner for two at a location of the old Steak and Ale chain, and our first night as a married couple, which we spent in the Adolphus Hotel in downtown Dallas. It didn't feel all that dramatic to be married—we'd been fully committed both emotionally and physically for almost four years—but we greatly looked forward to living together 24/7.

But by the time of our brief honeymoon, I was making a first move toward revealing my CD nature to Val. Firmly bound as I'd been to continued secrecy before the wedding, the fact of our marriage led to an abrupt change in my perspective. I was coming to realize that, now, the greatest danger to our relationship lay in further attempts to hide. It would be madness to attempt continued subterfuge. As a married adult, my access to "maybe it's just a phase" was gone. I was a cross-dresser, period, and would be one for life. And even if life wasn't perfect for Val and me, it was going to have to be real.

My honeymoon initiative was not a full opening up. I didn't admit to Val the depths of my feelings, nor was this a first step in any planned program. It came about rather serendipitously.

We departed for the honeymoon on January 2, after hanging around a couple days for the January 1 Cotton Bowl game in Dallas between Texas and Nebraska. Our destination was New Orleans, as exotic a spot as we could manage within the day's-drive limit Val's dad was requiring for the lend of his Ford Pinto. (We would buy a car within a couple weeks, but as yet we still had none.)

Our New Orleans motel was a dump, a place on the Airline Highway well out from the French Quarter and downtown. But, of course, we made it to Bourbon Street, and, big surprise, I was immediately attracted by the drag shows. I hadn't pushed for New Orleans because of that—I'm not sure I even knew the Quarter had such places—but what an incubator for my desires.

Here were men dressed as women, performing in a sexy setting with a very adult "two-drink minimum." The drag queens weren't quite cross-dressers like me, but I wasn't focused on such distinctions, and Valerie was

OK with it, perhaps because it was the sort of mildly scandalous thing you can do as a newly minted, pleasure-seeking grownup. I just had to hide the fact that once I saw these shows, the Crescent City's other attractions became secondary to me. And on our second night, I brought cross-dressing home to the motel.

Valerie was ready to shut it down by about eleven o'clock. We had been sightseeing all day and partying into the evening. But I was still awake after she was snoozing, and into the bathroom I went to get into her makeup. I exited wearing mascara and blue eye shadow. Valerie's makeup style didn't really lean toward blue shadow, but I had urged her long ago to get some because I liked it *on her*. Blue shadow was an early imprinter on me, seeming just so perfectly feminine.

I envisioned sex with my makeup on, hoping that Val would see it as kinky fun after what we'd witnessed in the shows. She didn't stir when I crawled into bed, though.

"Ohhh guyyy..." I crooned. "Guy" was a pet phrase we had called each other since college.

But I elicited only a mumble and decided it was best to just go to sleep myself. It would be fun to wake up in makeup, she wouldn't be in a fog, and morning sex was always good.

I slept lightly, nervously, and I was fully alert at her first stir. Shortly, she lay half-awake on her side, facing away from me. A familiar position for spoon-style cuddling.

But this time I hiked an arm and a leg over her, straddling her on all fours.

"Good morning, I love you, wake up," I said. "Look at my surprise."

It took 0.34 seconds to know this was going nowhere. Her eyes were pools of disbelief. She squinted and shook her head, as if to expel any last clouds of sleep.

"What did you do!" Her tone was more scold than question. "Are you wearing makeup? Jack, what is going on?"

"I just thought it you might think it would be fun. I got the idea from the drag shows. I thought it could be a new way to be sexy."

I spoke the spiel with little enthusiasm and no hope. It had sounded OK when composed ten hours previously, but this was now, and let's just say she wasn't in the mood. I might as well have suggested intercourse in the parking lot.

"No," she said. "No, I don't think that's sexy at all. I don't like it. I want you to look like you. Will you please take it off and not do it again?"

I've always been one to know when to cut my losses, so immediately I bailed. The mascara was washable, needing only a little soap. I returned to find my wife in her regular morning routine, and soon I was reassured that as badly as my gambit had bombed, my quick retreat would keep it from wrecking the rest of the honeymoon. I'd been cited only for a stupid moment, not for an inborn gender identity issue. We completed a good trip—though with no more trips to drag shows—and we drove back to Dallas a happy couple.

## CHAPTER 9

# CARVING A CAREER

L ife was a fine adventure dawning in January of 1974. I was not only a new adult and married, I was a married adult sportswriter. I was realizing my childhood goal of getting paid to attend ball games, even if only at the humble level of *The Arlington Daily News*, a suburban sheet in the Dallas–Fort Worth area. At least I had a toe in the door for a career that I knew could be a cheat-the-system choice for me.

"Seriously," a voice inside would whisper to me, "if you become a successful big-city sportswriter, will you not be constantly suppressing smirks, lest you let on to the Man that your job is just too damned much fun to merit a paycheck? You may not get rich, and yes, it's a bit competitive, but if you climb up that ladder just a bit, you could start netting not only a solid middle-class salary but also those incredible perks. Four-star travel to major games and events, with insider access a common fan could never sniff! The fans pay thousands to be there, but you'd be *getting* paid."

For a kid who always loved sports, always loved travel, and never loved working as hard as valedictorians do, this career was an object of lust. In my final semester in college, I volunteered for *The Daily Texan*, a top-ranked college paper, and it had sold me completely and permanently on these truths, once I successfully navigated a nerve-wrenching first day.

"We need a story out of football practice today," said the sports editor, Joe Phillips, on that October day. "Think you can go to the stadium and get that?"

Phillips was respected as a cool and capable sports guy, just like I wanted to be. But at this very moment, I couldn't help but question his judgment. Why would he trust me for this day's coverage of the nationally prominent Longhorns team? They were the lead sports story in Austin almost every single day, and I was nobody, just a kid in J-school who was belatedly volunteering at the paper after three years of spending my non-class hours goofing off. I still wonder about his thought process—maybe his proven reporters were all hungover—but 2:00 p.m. on that Tuesday found me walking from the J Building to the eighty-thousand-seat Memorial Stadium.

I needed a story with quotes from the coach and several players looking ahead to the next game, and I was also tasked with gathering any news of the day. I was confident I understood football well enough to get some material from watching practice, and I knew I could write. But of the reporting part, I was not so sure.

I would have the run of the locker room, coaches' offices, equipment room, and such. I just needed the pluck to find the people I needed in the warren of dark facilities under the stands.

When I found Darrell Royal, Texas's already legendary head coach, he was buck naked and dripping wet. I nearly ran into him as he bolted from a shower area while grumbling about a shortage of towels.

*The biggest name ever in Texas football*, I thought, *and he's two feet away from me in his birthday suit.*

Royal, who had already won three national championships and would eventually see Memorial Stadium rechristened with his name, seemed not at all upset over my being in his way. A lot of people were in a lot of people's ways in that labyrinth. But the downside was that Royal didn't give a damn who I was or why I was there, and in seconds he was stepping it down a hallway, pale white butt cheeks and all, with a white T-shirt and briefs in hand. I couldn't let him disappear on me.

"Coach Royal! I'm here from *The Daily Texan*. Do you have a minute?"

"Can you let me get my clothes on?" he barked.

Then he turned and looked at me and got nicer.

"Sure, son," he said. "Just knock on this door in five minutes."

Bingo. I would soon have comments from the absolute key element for my story. Royal proved cordial as can be, musing on the upcoming game and detailing some lineup changes, and then for me it was off to the players' locker room. I needed to find the quarterback—you always need the quarterback—and a couple of others.

I did it. It was time to write my story on old yellow copy paper in a manual typewriter. It took me two hours, more than a veteran would have needed, but when I handed it to Phillips, it was only 7:00 p.m., still several hours from the copy deadline for Wednesday's paper. Surely Phillips had to be braced for an unusable effort from his little-known correspondent, and my confidence was still so fragile that when he walked toward me after reviewing the story, my stomach started acting up.

But he said it was "fine," and massive waves of relief engulfed me.

In weeks to come, I would write Texas football game stories as well as sports opinion columns. I even made a road trip to San Antonio for a story on the pro basketball Spurs. The columns featured my name in huge letters, along with a silhouette image of my smiling face, framed in wild hair and a beard. I had a full blown Afro at the time, done with my consent and Val's approval by a friend of Val's with hairstyling skill. I liked looking rather the hippie, hoping it would further separate me from the business-major world of fraternity life.

On the days these columns were published, I no longer felt like just one of forty thousand on campus. Friends would note my work, and I felt for the first time the enchanting pull of being a media figure.

But when I started looking for a real sportswriting job, after earning my degree in December of 1973, I quickly came to feel like a nobody again. It was all too evident that I should have volunteered at *The Daily Texan* much sooner, because my file of byline stories from that one final senior semester was too thin to impress major sports editors. These guys cared far more about published work than my honors diploma, despite Texas's rating as a top journalism school.

My search proved so unproductive that I was led to pursue and accept a non-sports job, a news reporting assignment for *The Arlington Daily News*. I had to get some experience and earn a living. But fate smiled, because just after my agreement on a start date, the number-two guy in the two-man sports department exercised an option to claim the news reporting opening. I accepted his sports spot with glee.

In sports, the Arlington paper offered its sportswriters a plum that other suburban papers in the area couldn't match. Though our mission was "local news only," Arlington's local included Major League Baseball's Texas Rangers. Their stadium was in our city limits, sited there to attract fans from both Dallas to the east and Fort Worth to the west. Covering Rangers games afforded me the distinctive opportunity to get reamed out by their manager, the mercurial and combative Billy Martin, who won five World Series rings as a New York Yankee infielder before managing five different big-league teams over eighteen tumultuous years.

One night, as I looked to interview players in the clubhouse after a game, I found Martin charging toward me in a T-shirt, boxers, and rubber sandals, bellowing that I had tried to "spy" on him through a cracked doorway into his office. And indeed, our gazes had met just moments earlier as Martin peered through the crack from inside his sanctum. Reporters couldn't avoid occasionally glancing at his door while scanning the player lockers on either side of it, and the view had proven exceptionally eye-catching this night, because through the crack one could see Billy brutally chewing out somebody in a Rangers uniform, either a player or a coach. I had focused on that for perhaps 3.5 seconds before Martin's eyeballs suddenly blocked the view and laser-tracked toward mine.

It didn't matter that I had not sought out this visual. Nor did it matter that I had every right as a journalist to peer through that crack, as long as I did it from space the team had credentialed me to occupy. The *Daily News* was paying me for my powers of observation as well as for my writing, and Martin could have just closed his door, for gosh sakes. But still, I got a full verbal flogging from a man who ten years later would have his No. 1 jersey retired by the Yankees.

"I don't know who the hell you are, but you won't be in here again if I catch you spying on me one more time!" Martin bellowed.

"But I—"

"I don't want your damn excuses," Martin said. "If I were you, I'd stay away from me for a while."

It wasn't really that bad, though. It was rather a badge of honor in the local media to take a hit from fiery Billy, and it was a good first lesson in learning to be stoic with badly behaving sports celebrities.

Meanwhile, Valerie had found a job as a preschool teaching assistant. Like me, Val had entered college with a definite career goal. She had a gift for engaging with small children, and she sought a degree in her mom's field, early childhood education. She would work this job until the fall, when she would enroll at Texas Woman's University, some thirty miles north of Dallas, to complete her degree. She was a semester behind me in completing school, as I had been able to graduate in three and a half years, due to advanced placement credits out of Cistercian, mostly in French.

Our first apartment was in Dallas, in a sort of sexy-but-gritty neighborhood near downtown. We were hip enough to know it was what amounted to the "gay area," muted as that was at the time. As the first couple from our high school set to have our own place, we hosted numerous parties.

In September of '74 we moved some twenty miles west to the bedroom community of Euless, a mid-cities locale between Dallas and Fort Worth. I had a new and better sports job at *The Fort Worth Press*, a real city paper with a wire service for national and regional news. The move worked for Valerie, too, as she would still be able to finish her degree at Texas Woman's U.

I worked a lot of nights at the *Press*, and with Valerie a good distance away in school during the week, I encountered long days in an apartment in a not very walkable neighborhood. I was too far from Dallas for quick lunches or other short meetings with friends, and to pass the time I'd go to a local rec center with my basketball. But the place was mostly deserted on weekdays, and I remember many winter-gray days as quite boring.

You can likely guess what came to fill the gap.

## CHAPTER 10

# SHOPPING SHIVERS

By the time we moved to Euless, I had become a shopper. No more rummaging through a mother's or girlfriend's bureau. I wanted new and sexier things.

Girls had access to such a wide world of fashion and beauty. Sexy messaging and marketing were everywhere. But how was I to access it? How could I buy girly things and not be exposed as a queer?

My risk tolerance would have to rise. But still, there were limits. I needed to shop in gender-neutral stores and be furtive to the max. I needed clothing-and-merchandise places with a central checkout, like the Kmart where I had bought that first pair of heels. Kmart was big in Texas in the '70s, and though its clothes and shoes were rarely the stuff of a sexy sissy's wildest dreams, the camouflage factor of filling my cart with other items remained immensely helpful.

Once in a great while I'd break my rules and risk the women's area of a mall department store. My neighborhood JCPenney impressed me with a discreet and quietly welcoming sales staff, and I returned a time or two. But still it was quite a heart-pounder taking a skirt or blouse and nothing else to a women's counter, and I wouldn't consider shoes in any mall department store. Not only would this require interaction with a clerk who dealt only in women's shoes, department store layouts invariably had the shoes in places along the main aisles, wide open to the view of all patrons. One couldn't hide in Women's Shoes as well as in Junior Fashions.

But even at Kmart, a relaxed buy was impossible. I recall the fairly rare case of a very cute skirt on display. Silky, perfect length, girly stripes. It first caught my eye while I was in the store for "normal" reasons.

"You could buy that!" a voice within me said. "Right through the main checkout, easy does it, with a bunch of guy stuff."

"You can't risk it," countered a second voice. "Even if there's no problem at checkout, you'll have bought the wrong size and be embarrassed to return it. And it costs $18.95!"

But the first voice tended to prevail in such debates, and I was back two days later, on a mission.

Job one was to resurvey the women's section, identify my target, and then promptly leave for sporting goods or hardware. In that safe space I could pause and think about the items I would need in the basket before grabbing the skirt.

Those items secured, I returned to the area near the skirt as nonchalantly as possible, like a bored guy waiting for his girlfriend or wife. Upon detecting a probability that no one was looking, I snatched what I guessed would be my size and dropped it in my basket, staying on the move all the while. Then it was back to hardware to find a deserted aisle and arrange my items so that the skirt could be somewhat concealed without getting wrinkled.

Once near the checkouts, I had to stop again and watch, like a squirrel just down from a tree.

Did I see anyone who might know me? If so, I would flee for the back of the store to wait out their departure. Five minutes of this waiting would seem like fifty, as I'd begin worrying about possible questions from Valerie as to why my errands had taken so long.

This time the coast was clear, but there was more info to gather before I could brave checkout. Which of the female cashiers (males were never considered) looked the most benign and disinterested? Older was better, as was apparent unconcern for fashion. And once the best candidate was identified, I had to analyze the customers in her line. You can get trapped in a checkout lane, so I avoided shoppers I perceived as too friendly, too nosy, or too aggressively masculine—anyone who might note that "This guy is buying a skirt."

I tried to have a few lines in my head for an attempted explanation. Possibly that my sister knew I was coming to Kmart—for all this other stuff, including a goddamn quart of oil, yessir—and that she'd asked me to pick this up and told me where to find it.

No explanations were needed this time, but when I slumped into my car, I saw that seventy-five minutes had been needed to pick up a skirt and four other items. At least the skirt did fit. Size L.

Makeup and pantyhose were best bought at a grocery, as it was easy to identify plenty of other basket-fillers we routinely needed, and usually I was willing to risk two feminine items. But often I needed three or four, and it would look just too funny for a guy to be buying mascara, eye shadow, eyeliner, *and* pressed powder. Alarm bells might sound. Extra store trips, each with its own set of regular merchandise, were often required to get what I needed.

Years later, with more confidence and freedom, I would realize that shopping need not be a fearful experience. It would dawn, as I became more confident going out, that shopping en femme was absolutely the way for a sissy to go.

I've almost never been hassled while shopping dressed, and not only is it less stressful, it's much more effective because I can rifle the racks without worrying who's looking, and I can also *try things on*. I recall only one time when a store employee—a dour Steinberg's lady—told me I had to use the men's fitting rooms. No female customer has ever complained about me being in women's rooms, and I have been in many where moms were helping their teen or even preteen daughters try things on. Despite the efforts of cultural right-wingers to raise fears about predatory transgender folks in fitting rooms or bathrooms, it's my experience that women under sixty in relatively progressive areas simply do not perceive a threat.

But all that good stuff about shopping en femme was years away for me when we lived in Euless. The hard way in male garb was the only way to shop, and I couldn't afford to find myself saying, "I just don't have a thing to wear!" Because new opportunities for dressing were at hand.

# ALONE WITH MY THINGS

During our nine-month stay in Euless, I dressed more often, more completely, and for longer periods than ever before. I had my first-ever real trove of girl things, hidden with great care inside our tiny apartment, a one-bedroom box in a complex that resembled a giant motel. Though venturing out the front door en femme remained but a pipe dream, I was happy enough with my growing collection and the extended blocs of private time Val's school schedule was providing.

I would dress as if I actually were going out, thrilled to be wearing nothing masculine while donning underthings, hose, and heels, a skirt-and-blouse or dress, and full makeup. I improved my skill at creating a figure with socks stuffed in my bra. But the one thing I noticeably still lacked was a wig. I just couldn't figure out how to safely attain one, as it seemed they were available only at wig stores, where I wasn't brave enough to go. The possibility of mail order was just not in my thoughts. What if Valerie picked up the mail?

But the mind is darned good at ignoring what it wants to, and at this stage of my CD development, I could block out more than just my male haircut. For a time after my very hairy college days I still had a full beard, yet when dressing time came, I'd manage not to see all those bristles and still somehow think I looked pretty.

Aside from being dressed, I was likely not so different from other guys of twenty-two with a day to kill at home. I'd watch TV, listen to music, smoke pot, and eat. Maybe even read a while. But I admired myself incessantly in the mirror. I'd get feeling really sexy, and I'd fantasize.

I'd start with just the idea of being outside that apartment. The same basic fantasy I'd had at three and a half about wearing Janie's blouse around the neighborhood. I'd imagine what it would be like to stroll the sidewalk or even go to the grocery. Those things would never happen, I knew, but I also knew I'd always wish they somehow could.

I might also imagine being forced out of the closet by a dominant superior. How about two or three mean girls who somehow held sway over me? I'd be totally scorned and humiliated when these hot and sexy meanies took me to my high school reunion, perfumed and rouged and in heels. What would the guys say about me? How horrible and scary and sexy to contemplate! This is a common fantasy theme in cross-dressing fiction, which I read at the time when I could get my hands on it.

The "good" reasons for accepting my true nature as a CD—self-affirmation, genuineness, overcoming fear—were largely lost on me as a very young adult. It was all about sexual arousal behind closed doors. I cultivated the idea of being attractive to men. I imagined several girlfriends helping me get all pretty for a date they had set up for me. "He is gonna *love* this dress on you," one would say. Then I'd wonder how it would feel when the guy and I were in the car alone together. To think he would see me as sexy, as I sat very close to him, was exciting. I imagined, ultimately, having sex with a man.

I didn't identify as homosexual, however. When I'd see two studs and two babes in a TV ad, I'd be looking exclusively at the babes. The guys were just furniture. The girls would be sexy as hell, designed to give straight males a rise, and there was straight male within me for sure. I had no hard-wired connection to finding men attractive and no interest in sex with a man *as a man myself.* But if it would come as part of an ultimate dressing experience, I was not at all repulsed by the concept.

That was my truth, and as I learned more traditional psychology about cross-dressing, I came to perceive a disconnect between myself and the CDs I read about.

The information I found strongly supported the idea that most CDs were "exclusively heterosexual," even when in skirts. The arrow on their libido meter was said to be pointed 100 percent toward women and zero towards men.

But it was hard for me to imagine the love of lipstick not leading other CDs to fantasize about flirting with and even submitting to a man. It wasn't something I planned to actually pursue—monogamy was the bedrock of marriage—but my fantasies were undeniably engaged.

Late during the Euless period, I made a stunning discovery. Good old Kmart, of all places, was offering a ravishing platinum-blonde wig. I still had yet to even try on any kind of wig, much less own one, and of course I just had to have it. My camouflage shopping system was put to a severe test by this explosively feminine item, but somehow I made it through checkout and excitedly returned to our apartment.

Then it hit me. I hadn't given it a thought. Motherfucking son of a bitch, I still had a goddamn beard.

*Shave it off. Shave it off right now.*

This was of a signature brand of CD moments. The instant when a bold and even shocking desire blindsides you like a runaway minivan. When your heart is suddenly thudding and you feel high. When devil-may-care becomes your MO and for once you just do what you want to do, fuck the world if it doesn't like it. You'll deal with that later.

Not that shaving a beard amounted to a public declaration of queerness, but still it was radical. I was yielding to dressing's demand that facial hair was unacceptable, making a snap decision on a big change in appearance, and as this was coming out of the blue, it would certainly require some careful explanation to Valerie. But this moment—this wild-seeming CD moment—was everything! My CD side was exercising total control.

I was as whacked out as Sweeney Todd as I slashed my whiskers for my first clean-shaven face in several years. I was mesmerized by the prospect of a look in the mirror at that new face surrounded by girly blonde locks.

Lipstick! I had no time to do full makeup, but lipstick would do a lot in a jiffy. Then I pulled on my first-ever wig.

It was awesome. Magnificent. Unprecedented. A worthy co-landmark to that first-ever feel of high heels. A plausible girl's face—well, almost—

stared back at me from the glass. At that point there was but one thing left to do: masturbate.

After which came the usual massive letdown. As I cleaned up, I pondered explaining to Valerie my sudden decision to shave. But beyond that specific issue, I was hit by feelings that I shouldn't have the wig at all. At $30, it had been a big purchase for a young sportswriter making $155 per week, and clearly it marked a new level of commitment to dressing. I worried that my urges held me captive in a bad way—maybe I really was just an icky queer after all—and I looked again at the wig. I felt the need to rid myself of it immediately, so I put it in a plastic bag, headed for the car, and drove it to a dumpster.

That evening, I tried to take the all-positive approach with Val about the shave.

"Close your eyes," I said from the kitchen as she walked in the front door. "I've got a surprise for you."

She did as instructed, and I stepped around the corner.

"Oh my goodness," she said. "I didn't even recognize you for a second. It was scary. You never told me you were planning to shave."

"It was spur of the moment," I said. "I just decided I was tired of the facial hair."

Which was entirely and absolutely true, though lacking a bit in context.

"What do you think? Do you like it OK?"

"Let's see," she said, nuzzling me cheek-to-cheek. "Yeah, that feels nice. I like it fine. It was just such a surprise."

So that part hadn't turned out too badly. But the very next morning, after Val had left for school, I was led to reevaluate the pros and cons of wig ownership. And after T-charting briefly, I was back at the dumpster, digging. I was living proof of the CD truth that guilt-induced "purges" never have staying power.

I felt pressure to work fast, as the dumpster was marked "KEEP OUT" in big letters. But I could not find the damn thing. Though I allotted myself only about fifteen minutes, for fear of attracting security, it seems to this day that the rescue should have been doable. There was no evidence of a major new dump since the day before. But twenty-four hours after its purchase, the wig was bringing me nothing but the feeling I was a fool.

I didn't toss out any more of my stuff. Maybe I had formed an intention to do so when I was in purge mode, but so quickly had my thoughts on the wig reversed themselves, the rest of my trove remained safe and still desired. I was mad at myself and mad at the culture that suppressed me, but as always, my generally positive self-concept emerged undamaged. I knew I couldn't change.

But a sea change regarding life with Valerie was fast upon me.

# THE CD LIFE: BLONDE

Gentlemen prefer them, Hollywood once told us, and when dressing, I certainly prefer to be one.

Nothing is more alluring to me as a female statement than spun-gold blonde hair. Of course, I'm speaking only of my personal sissy desires, but to me, blonde hair is it. High heels might be more bold—there's just no explaining away your sissiness wearing those—but the hair on one's very head is unmatched as a 24/7 statement to the world.

Pure blonde hair seems such a sudden jump on the color spectrum from ash blonde shades, much more starkly separated than black is from brown. And though bleached blonde hair can sometimes look less than natural, that can be a big femme kick in itself if you're bold enough to pull it off.

I wasn't sure I could ever pull off going blonde—my first wig was, but I had it so briefly it almost didn't count. Around 2013 I finally decided to try. I was comfortable by this time going dressed to a wig store, and when I tried on a particularly sassy blonde number, I knew I was going to give it a go.

Was I nervous? Of course. Don't women always fear epically bombing with a serious hairdo change? And this wig was not only very blonde, it was well shorter than anything I'd worn previously, going down only to the base of my male hairline. It was also asymmetrical, with much more hair and curls on the right side than on the left. But the several comments I received at the bar were all positive, and from that night on there was never a doubt I would wear blonde wigs more often than my darker ones. Shortly thereafter I purchased a slightly longer and more conservative blonde wig, affording me a powerful one-two punch.

It's not only the Marilyn Monroes of the world that make blondeness so attractive. In one 2017 study by Augsburg University, 110 men were shown photos of the same women with different computer-generated hair colors. The study found that blondes were considered younger and healthier looking, were more likely to be approached in social situations, and were more likely to be offered help from men than women with darker hair.

I think I'll grow my own hair long and dye it blonde. Just kidding. For now.

## CHAPTER 12

# TELLING VALERIE

I n the early spring of 1975, fifteen months after my blue eye shadow moment on our honeymoon, I opened up fully to Valerie. I'm glad I sensed only vaguely what I'd later come to know better—that cross-dressing can and does break up marriages. More knowledge might have scared me away.

The CD experience is aptly described as "usually intensely private and lonely." That's from an online article titled "Why Do Straight Men Cross-Dress?" and though I've already noted my skepticism about the overall straightness of CDs, I'll accept "straight men" in this title as applying to all CDs trying to live some kind of conventional life. The secrecy aspect, for sure, is inseparable from cross-dressing. Drag queens are never about hiding it; CDs almost always are.

The article notes that though CDs are often "tired of living in secrecy as their cross-dressing needs intensify, they find their spouse is often devastated, and the marriage seldom lasts after the secret is let out."

I see the phrase "marriage seldom lasts" as possibly too strong, since it's a premise of this narrative that married CDs are spread at least thinly among us, and likely not all in hiding from their wives. Even so, the gloomier assessment of dressing as a marriage-wrecker has been validated to me by conversations with other CDs at conventions, bars, and support groups.

The trauma of the "devastated spouse" has been described to me much as it's described in the article.

But by realizing at a still early stage that I couldn't keep hiding my nature, I gave our relationship a chance. I knew that without a full reckoning, our situation would only deteriorate. Though my coming out had the potential to put our relationship on the rocks, there would never be a better time to do it, likely only worse. I foresaw that even if I managed to keep my secret to the very end—with one of us literally at death's door—I would suffer grave second thoughts about the precious life energy I had spent in hiding the truth, about the richness and relational honesty that could have grown instead.

Valerie and I were in bed late at night with the light out when I delivered the news. We were still in our small apartment in Euless. I hadn't formed a plan to do it exactly then. I was dwelling on a trip we had made to a mall that day, thinking about some pretty clothes I had seen in a department store. I was feeling frustrated about how difficult and expensive it would be to obtain them, and how even if I did, I wouldn't be able to wear them in any way except alone in front of a mirror. My need to tell Valerie about myself had already been on a constant low burn for a couple weeks, and these torturous thoughts about dressing pushed me into action. I could tell that Val was not yet sleeping, either, so I launched in.

"Do you remember the night on our honeymoon when I put on your blue eye shadow?"

"Sort of," she replied. "I know I didn't like it and I asked you to take it off."

"Well, if you're still awake enough, there's something I need to tell you about that. It's been on my mind lately, and I don't think it's good to keep holding it in."

"I'm awake," she abruptly replied. "What?"

"Well, that eye shadow deal was not the first time I've done something like that. I know it must sound strange, but ever since I was a tiny kid, I've had urges to dress like a girl. So sometimes I do, just in private."

"Are you telling me after all this time together that you wish you were a girl?"

"No, not really. I think of myself as a guy, and I want to be a guy, and I want to be your husband and have a life together with you. But I'm this other way, too, sometimes. So I figured I'd better tell you because I don't want there to be a big secret between us."

"This sounds really strange. It scares me," she said. "What am I supposed to say when you dump this all on me late at night when I'm almost asleep? Can't you just stop? Can't you just not do it anymore?"

"I don't know," I said. "There have been periods since we met when I haven't done it. But the urge always comes back, and it's been back for a while now. I think it would be really hard to never do it again."

"So what do you do? When do you do it? What am I supposed to do? I don't even know what I'm supposed to say. I don't understand."

Did she cry? Did I cry? Yes, on both counts. It was agonizing. My tone was humble and our voices were hushed. She had more questions—Did I have my own clothes? Did anybody else know?—but she seemed to be just flailing and not that interested in the answers. She mostly said, again and again, that she didn't understand. Finally we agreed that there was no point in continuing all night. We nestled side-by-side, uneasily at first, but in time we both slept.

My ability to relax despite the stress was keyed by one overriding factor: amid all our emotional and sometimes confused talk, the prospect of our marriage ending had not come up.

Not to say Valerie took it in stride. She was clearly blown away. Valerie has always been guileless, and though there's a babe-in-the-woods cluelessness attached to that term in common usage, Webster tells us that guileless folk are "free from cunning, deception, or duplicity; sincere, honest, straightforward, and frank." I see Valerie's character in that light, so what a match for her to be coupled to a CD, a species often terrorized by King Culture into being, well, cunning, deceptive, and duplicitous.

I think Valerie had no more than the barest conception that there were men like me. She knew about drag queens but not about married guys who hide it. And now she suddenly knew she was wedded to one.

Her defense mechanism was to deep-six the whole thing. Like myself at various times, she probably worked to convince herself that it would somehow phase out.

One might ask how much I really knew about myself at this crucial stage. Not so much, perhaps, but at least I had known since about age fourteen that I was not alone on the planet. I had read of cross-dressing in one of the Dallas newspapers, in an Ann Landers advice column responding to a young woman's concern over her boyfriend's suggestion that they go out together as females. Ann explained that "Dale" was a "transvestite"—a now out-of-date term for cross-dressers—and she advised that he might benefit from some counseling. I don't think Ann advised the woman to summarily dump Dale, but I just don't remember. What I do remember, like it was yesterday, was the flashbulb going off in my head.

"That guy is me," I mused.

But some nine years after my acceptance of a CD identity, my admission to Valerie had provided her only puzzlement and worry. I accepted as inconceivable any idea that my dressing could become part of our life together. This was so out of bounds, in the context of the culture that reared us, that Valerie had zero second thoughts about the immediate way forward. We just wouldn't talk about it, and she would assume she would never have to see the reality I had described. If she didn't have to see it, she wouldn't have to think about whether it was happening.

I didn't think seriously about trying to persuade her to talk about it more. I didn't see the point, didn't know where the conversation might be able to go. If she accepted what I had told her and was ready to move on with our normal routines, I was not going to risk busting up that bit of serenity.

At least I wasn't hiding the reality anymore, and I made no vows to myself to quit. I didn't really believe I could, despite my largely conventional plans for my life. Where it would all go from here was just too big a load to process.

CHAPTER 13

# A SUDDEN MOVE

My Fort Worth sportswriting job had started with much promise. Six months in, I was promoted from high schools to covering Texas Christian University, which regularly played big-time opponents in football and basketball despite having generally poor teams of its own. But just two months later, the fifty-three-year-old *Press* closed its doors. It was an afternoon paper, a media species on its way to full extinction, and its demise had been speculated for a decade or more. Even in its better years, the *Press*'s circulation numbers had lagged far behind the rival *Fort Worth Star-Telegram*. But still, the actual crash happened out of the blue, employees learning on Thursday, May 29, 1975, that the Friday, May 30 edition would be the last.

Well, *most* employees learned it on Thursday. I didn't find out until Sunday, because the reach of media in the '70s didn't carry this story to Baltimore, where Valerie and I had spent the week visiting her dad's family. It had been my first-ever week of paid vacation. We belatedly got the word when our homeward journey took us by the Pilot home en route to our apartment.

"You don't have a job anymore!"

That was Theo's way to handle a tense message, just blurting it out with a laugh as we hit their doorstep. Then she gave me a hug.

"We thought about calling you," she said, "but we didn't want to ruin the end of your vacation."

I don't know if anyone at the *Press* thought to call, but in those days, even if someone had, they likely had been quite unsure how to reach me.

When I went to the quiet *Press* newsroom on Monday, I found a ragged piece of newsprint lodged in my typewriter carriage, scrawled with the message, "Jack—Don't bother sending out your column for Wednesday." It was classic dark journalism humor from a colleague. But I didn't face unemployment. By day's end it was settled that we would move to Memphis, where Scripps-Howard, owner of the *Press*, had found me another position. I would write sports for the ornately named *Memphis Press-Scimitar,* another afternoon paper, again number two in its town.

Coincidentally, I had passed through Memphis for the first two times on our drive to Baltimore and back. It wouldn't have been my first choice for a relocation, but I was like a young ballplayer suddenly traded. Memphis was now my route up the ladder, and I promptly made a solo move, lodging for three weeks with some distant relations. Val stayed back to finish her final degree work. It was a strange and lonely time for us, and it was a joy to be reunited when I returned to fetch her. But when we approached the Memphis outskirts she broke into tears, bereft over leaving her family for the first time, and matters only worsened when she saw the apartment I'd selected for us.

I had screwed that up royally, choosing a rather blighted part of town, known as Frayser, to get some extra room at a low price. I'd been overly swayed by a patch of green space outside the back door, as I longed to have a yard. The place overall wasn't nice, even by Frayser standards. An adjoining complex erected a chain link fence between the properties a few months after we arrived, and it was seven feet high with barbed wire on top—angled toward our side like a prison yard.

While Valerie was able to find a preschool teaching job she liked and forgave my lack of real estate acumen in time, my job was not working out as planned.

"Jack, I need to talk to you right now."

This was December 1975, some six months after I'd started at the *Press-Scimitar.* My boss, sports editor George Lapides, was about to reduce me to tears.

No one in the sports department liked George. He was a bully, a braggart, and a petty tyrant. We talked about him constantly when he wasn't around, and everyone got abused by him at least occasionally. We derisively called him the "Big Chief," and to describe days in the office when he *wasn't* around, I coined an acronym that remains in use today, some forty years later, among our still-tight group of former staffers: "NRDWBC," meaning "a nice relaxing day without the Big Chief."

But even as George would be reaming out the other guys, he seemed to implicitly respect them as worthy at least of continued employment by the company. To me, this affirmation was not accorded.

I guess George had personally hired all or most of the others. But I had been forced on him by the Scripps-Howard bosses seeking spots for *Fort Worth Press* refugees. And I was not just a bonus body added to his staff. I was filling a hole created when a respected veteran sports staffer accepted a transfer to news side.

I didn't blame George for being pissed about having a hire snatched from his hands, but he was the absolute worst kind of boss for such a situation. I didn't get a compliment or pat on the back about anything for six months, and on this day when we "needed to talk," he was yanking me from my main reporting assignment, the entry-level position of covering Memphis high schools.

"We're not real happy with what we're getting from you," George said. "I was right that this wouldn't be good for our department. You're not that good of a writer, and you're sure not working very hard."

The former charge was a matter of opinion, I suppose, but the latter was a canard. I had a burning desire to succeed in this field, and my current raison d'être was getting promoted from high schools to a college beat, like the one I'd been about to have in Fort Worth. I came in every day wanting to work hard and produce.

But George was less interested in using my energy than in showing everyone what a terrible injustice had been foisted upon him. He found that sometimes, during a natural lull in an overnight editing shift that all staffers had to work occasionally, I would turn on the department TV and watch the 7:00 a.m. news. I'd be right there if the supervising editor needed anything, and it would be too early to be making any calls on the high school beat. But those factors didn't save me.

"We're putting you full-time on the overnight shift," George said, "and don't let me hear of you turning on that TV. This'll free up our good writers from having to work that shift, and maybe you can learn a few things in the meantime. You should be glad you're still getting this chance. Some people here would fire you in this situation."

George offered zero encouragement that I could hope to climb back up the ladder. He again disparaged my writing ability, saying that success in the Memphis market—about three levels more elite in his mind than in mine—would be a real stretch for me. He had issued my demotion as I was completing one of those graveyard shifts that were now to be my nightly lot, and after trudging into that crappy first apartment of ours about 9:30 a.m., with Valerie already gone for the day, I sat on our bed and just cried, both devastated and angry.

"I don't know how to even face the other people in the newsroom," I told Valerie that evening. "I'm nothing but a glorified copy clerk now."

"From what you've told me before," she offered, "those other people probably understand what you're dealing with. George, I mean."

In any event, I wouldn't be seeing many coworkers while toiling from 12:30 to 8:30 a.m. Even worse, it was winter, and it quickly became evident that if I followed a natural inclination to sleep for eight hours upon returning home in the morning, it would be 5:30 p.m. and dark when I awoke. I'd be spending all my waking hours in darkness. I compensated by sleeping a split shift, forcing myself up by 3 p.m. and later snoozing for two more hours before heading to work.

With my background in the much larger sports market of Dallas–Fort Worth, it particularly galled me to be treated like the class dunce in the nation's weakest sports town for a city its size. Memphis was the country's least affluent major metro area and the largest without a major pro team. The only hot ticket in town was Memphis State University basketball, which shortly before my arrival had risen as far as a loss to UCLA and Bill Walton in the NCAA championship game. The town hungered mightily for top-level college football, entranced by the prestigious Southeastern Conference, but the only hometown team was Memphis State, a lackluster independent. The city's ardent attempts to lure an NFL team had always gone nowhere, and though Memphis strongly supported a "World Football League" team that signed away some big NFL names, the league as a whole folded after only a couple years. Bottom line, I had to escape this town.

I did only minimal cross-dressing during this demotion period. My feelings were not unlike what they had been during those high school years when I was desperate to gain a foothold in the conventional dating scene. I had seen dressing to be an impediment in that quest, and though there was no direct conflict between dressing and searching for a new job, I was now so desperate to get my career out of its tailspin that I saw dressing as a drain on precious time and energy. I thought of it less often, for a time. The urge would await a better stage in my guy's life before returning.

## CHAPTER 14

# THINGS GET BETTER

Just as I never felt despoiled about being a CD, I never lost confidence in my sportswriting ability. I knew my demotion was the result of George's personal axe to grind, and I stuck it out. And just like the queer mantra "things get better," eventually things got better for me.

I did scads of cold-call job applications to newspapers all over the country, but I got only pat-on-the-back responses, no offers. In the meantime, George's urge to ruin me started to fade a bit. Reinstated to the high school beat in 1977, I exposed a football team that cheated to win a close game. The coach had a star player illegally switch jersey numbers just before a crucial play, and he shielded it from the referees by lining up other players on the bench to block the refs' view from the field. But I saw it clear as day, and after the cheating team scored a decisive touchdown with its trickery, its machinations were reported at the top of our sports section the next day, complete with some transparently evasive comments I pried from the cheating coach. The morning paper also had a reporter at the game, but he got none of the real story.

In early 1978, George assigned me to cover the rebirth of pro baseball in Memphis, a fairly big deal. Though the city had a rich history as minor leagues went, the '70s had been the pits, with a stretch of poorly run teams followed by a '77 season with no team at all. New ownership cleverly promoted 1978 as a return to past glory, with several fallen traditions reinstated, and my stories received good play on our pages.

Around this time, my closet door also cracked open just a bit. We were free from our eighteen-month lease on the Frayser apartment, and we became homeowners in the solidly middle-class Raleigh neighborhood, about twelve miles northeast of downtown.

The first significant event was a visit to our Raleigh home by one of Val's cousins. Travis "Vic" McClinton was a year older than Valerie and me at twenty-six and had been frequently in Val's life during her Waco childhood. He had been out as gay since around the time of our marriage, and the extended family, though largely conservative, had handled it just as you'd hope a loving clan would, welcoming him as always. Maybe that should have encouraged me that my coming out to everyone wouldn't be so bad. But it never entered my mind.

Vic lived in Dallas as an adult and was in Memphis for some kind of queer people's convention. Good for Memphis, that it could host such a thing at that time. It seemed a rather bold concept, and Vic was all in, planning to stay several days.

Then my idea alarm went off. The inner flash left me lightheaded for a moment. This was a chance that might never recur. It was worth the peril of a try.

I looked for a time when Valerie seemed loose and happy. It came on a Friday evening when she was headed out with two unmarried girlfriends, fellow instructors at her preschool. They occasionally shared pitchers of beer at a place where they liked to play pool, and I never complained. For one thing, these evenings offered me dressing time.

"Oh, guy," I said. "What day did you say Vic was coming?" I knew already, but it seemed the best opener.

"Tuesday," she said. "Tuesday late."

"Well, I was thinking about doing something while he's here. I know you might not be crazy about it, but it would mean a lot to me..."

"What?" She had not been paying full attention, preoccupied with changing out a purse. But plunging ahead was the only option, and I determined to have my full say without interruption.

"Well, I know you don't much want to be around me when I dress up, but sometimes I'd just like to not be alone, and I thought maybe I could get dressed one night around Vic. It's not like he'd think it was so weird. He knows we accept him, and he'd accept me, and he wouldn't be off trying to tell everybody about it. I'll only do it this one time with him and I'm not pressing to do anything else down the road."

That last disclaimer would be borne out over time as risible, but at that moment I didn't foresee it. There was no past nor future in my CD mindset. It was another of those signature moments. Being able to dress for Vic's visit was everything.

"I don't know," she said. "Why do you bring stuff like this up when I'm busy with something else? I'm getting ready to leave right now. We'll talk about it later. I don't really think that's a great idea, though."

We kissed lightly.

"Have a good time," I said, and I did so with a smile, because I knew she would let me do it. Valerie liked Vic, always had, and there was a spring to her step as she headed to meet her friends. So obviously I had not rocked her world too severely, and hopefully all I needed was a little patience.

"If you really want to dress up for Vic, I guess I'm not going to try to stop you," she said the next day after lunch.

We were side-by-side at the kitchen sink, doing dishes. She said it looking straight ahead, impassively, without breaking rhythm on a pot scrub. Such was often her way of abruptly getting back to uneasy matters left hanging.

Inside me, fireworks. But outside, just a nod and a "Thank you."

She felt she'd earned a pass on the rest of the dishes, striding purposefully for her easy chair in the adjoining living room.

"Just don't make me have to have anything to do with it," she called over her shoulder.

Over dinner, she brought it up again.

"It sounds like he won't get here till late," she said, "and I've got work Wednesday morning. So I'll just go to bed a little early and let you meet him. Tell him I'll see him Wednesday afternoon. I'm not really happy about this, though. Please don't be loud."

I quickly moved to neutral topics. It felt restorative to my manhood to remind her I had a softball game on Wednesday, and the less we talked now about Vic, the less the chance for some crushing reversal on her part. But I was thinking only of Tuesday night, when I would finally cease kinship with the Elephant Man, Gregor Samsa, and similar wretches whose ghastly abnormality was simply not to be countenanced by others.

Vic would be only the second person on earth to know of me, as well as being the first with whom I'd actually interact. I came out to Vic in a phone call and easily gained his approval of my plan.

"It should be fun," he decided.

On Tuesday evening, I had only about an hour before Vic's estimated arrival. I'd have preferred ninety minutes at least, but my makeup went on without incident, and I had premodeled my outfit—a tan pleated skirt, rather modest, and a flowing brown rayon blouse. I loved shiny blouses; they were so unmistakably not male. I had purchased my outfit—tremblingly—at the neighborhood JCPenney.

Also by this time, I had a couple wigs that had avoided death in a dumpster. Valerie had come to accept that I would occasionally receive female things by mail, and I had ordered wigs from the Paula Young catalog, though I always considered it a splurge. I favored light brown colors, seeking styles that would frame my face to look slim. I wondered how I'd survived so long without some pretty female hairdos.

I was excited that this time that pretty face would be seen by more than just my own eyes in a mirror. When I arose to respond to Vic's knock, I felt my female persona becoming real as never before. Not that I felt like I'd suddenly become 100 percent a woman—my brain just didn't work that way—but suddenly I was real as a man who loved to present as a girl.

"Well, you look real cute," Vic said upon entering. I didn't know whether he really meant it or was just trying to be nice. How did I know how I'd look to someone else? Given Valerie's "I don't wanna see it" mindset, it was essentially true that *no one had ever seen me.*

But regardless of what Vic really thought, his intention had been kind. After I acknowledged his compliment, it seemed neither of us much knew what more to say about my reveal. Though I'd seen and talked with Vic many times in family situations, this was probably our first one-on-one conversation. We made a move to more familiar ground and stayed on a pleasant but quotidian track. He didn't ask many questions about dressing, and I didn't offer much. My primary thought the whole time was "Damn, here I am in a skirt, actually talking to someone who knows I really like to wear skirts."

Vic had rented his own room near the convention, and he decamped for there around midnight. I gave him a little hug and confirmed that Valerie and I planned to meet him at the convention the next day. Ostensibly, we simply wanted to spend time with him, but having moved toward acceptance that I was queer myself, I was interested on my own account. Vic was doing me a huge service, providing me cover to check this out. (I never thanked him for that, and I should have. He died of cancer, at age fifty, in 2001.)

I pondered with intense interest what the convention would be like. Would it offer anything specific for CDs? I had just about determined that it wouldn't, and we were walking toward the exit when I saw it. A booth where the "women" clearly were men. I suppose in retrospect that some of them could have been trans women rather than CDs, but actual trans people were not really on culture's radar in 1980. I did know about Christine Jorgensen, but she seemed an isolated and faraway case, so at this time I assumed without conjecture that these folks were cross-dressers like me. They were encased in feminine finery from head to toe in rather a traditional fashion, almost as if they were headed to church on a Sunday morning. But the detail of their outfits was insufficient for them to pass, and surely they knew that. Yet they were undeterred.

It was a stunning visual, my first in-the-flesh confirmation that I was not alone in my strange ways. Of course I knew that from things I'd read, starting with that Ann Landers column more than a decade earlier, but the impact of actually seeing other CDs far outstripped what words or pictures could do. Here were live humans who had gone miles farther down the CD road than I had yet to even imagine.

What were they like? Were they regular guys like me when they weren't en femme, or did they act gay and girly all the time? What were the life circumstances that allowed them to be out in public like this? Even if they were safe at this event, how had they navigated here? Were any of them married like me, or did their advanced proclivities indicate they had no real life outside of petticoats?

None of those answers would come my way, because this experience was still off-limits to me. The booth, perhaps thirty-five yards away, was not on our path toward the exit, and the idea of anything more than a glance from afar was not to be entertained. Valerie and Vic seemed not to notice the booth at all, and despite them knowing what they knew, I was not about to let on what I was experiencing. Even had I been alone, at this point in my journey I likely would have shied from a closer approach. It was good to see these folks and to learn they had a support group of some kind, but I was just not ready for it. It hurt that I wasn't; I yearned so badly for something more, but in mere seconds we were out the door and back on the streets of Straight World. Val and I would make this our only convention visit, leaving Vic to do his thing solo for the next couple days.

But perhaps the pent-up energy from that encounter played a part in Memphis becoming the place where I bought my first pair of really killer heels. The experience of getting those shoes, though, would prove some of my greatest fears correct.

# THE CD LIFE: EYES

The eyes have it. Or if they don't, take another look at your makeup.

You need maximum-impact eyes to balance the strong statement your lipstick is making. Because it's difficult to do, beautiful eye makeup is a dividing line between accomplished sissies and merely aspiring ones.

The proof is in the precision. Beautiful eyes begin not with mascara or shadow, but with thin yet bold strokes of eyeliner, both under the eye and on your upper lash line. A great application of liner may not be self-evident when your eyes are fully done, but without it you're like a quarterback trying to score without a good offensive line. To fully see eyeliner's impact, line one eye, with no other makeup, and leave the other eye bare. The lined eye will pop out dramatically.

I favor liquid liner over pencils, but not the kind with a flimsy little brush you dip in a bottle. There's too little control with that, and this is an area where errors cannot be tolerated. The way to go is with an eyeliner pen, which dispenses liquid liner through a very sharp but cushiony tip. It's like a Flair pen for makeup. It works great, and one eight-dollar pen seems to last forever. Given their price and performance, and the essential service they provide, I would rate these pens among the best bargains in all sissy-dom. I've had them from Maybelline and L'Oréal.

Mascara isn't as difficult to apply as liner, but it requires precision as well. You want your lashes to be longer and fuller than anyone's wildest dreams—every time—but one wayward stroke can cost you ten minutes with a cover stick and still leave you feeling like you look smudged and crappy. Most mascaras seem to work best when you apply a reasonable amount, let it dry, and then come back with additional coats. Lower lashes are almost as tricky as doing eyeliner, because they're right there next to your skin and can handle only a small amount of mascara per coat. This dictates patience, as your coats don't really start to show until about the third one. It's hard to maintain your application discipline when the strokes don't seem to be accomplishing anything, but an artful sissy learns to have faith.

You can easily spend twelve to fifteen bucks on drugstore mascaras, including styles that include two tubes, one containing "extending fibers" that you brush on while lashes are still wet from a first coat of the regular stuff. But here's a bottom line for the budget conscious: Most mascaras overpromise their results. Their "new looks" are just the same stuff in new packaging, and you can have very good lashes every time from a six-buck bottle of Maybelline Great Lash.

Eye shadow is relatively easy, although it's key to line the crease behind your eyelid with a darker shade than your lid shade. This provides depth. Pretty shades for your lids are always terribly tempting, blues and teals especially, but you must restrain yourself from putting on too much of these. It can make your eyes look cartoony and actually smaller. Even though it looks less spectacular going on, the subtle and smoky sexiness of gray lid color is a winner every time, with black creasing and highlights.

A singular frustration of mine is that never once, in countless career tries, have I successfully applied false eyelashes. For me, they are just too flimsy, impossible to affix at the lash line where they look somewhat natural. A few times I've managed to get one on acceptably, but never both. So I just try to compensate with more mascara, envying the female anchors on cable news when they bat their eyes and show those big, thick lashes.

## CHAPTER 15

# NEW AND BOLDER VENTURES

The Memphis killer heels experience began when I spotted the marvelous footwear in a mall, at Baker's, a shoe chain that catered only to women. They were strappy and spiky and a gleaming patent-leather white, artfully suspended at a fetching angle in a display window. I wanted them so badly—I unquestionably *had to have them*—that I was ready for an unprecedented risk.

This wasn't Kmart, where the shoes were self-service. That experience was scary enough, but at Baker's I would have to ask a clerk for the specific style in a certain size and then get the hell out as quickly as possible. I'd have to pray I could escape massive humiliation with the flimsy, unspoken premise that I must be buying them for someone else.

I was hyped as high as I thought possible upon entering the mall, but my anxiety rose further as I did a Baker's pass-by. The clerk was male—very bad news—and, even worse, about my age. Plus, there were other customers inside, including one other man, not a queer like me but clearly with his wife or girlfriend. But I wasn't turning back. I attempted a purposeful and manly stride to the counter and spoke to the clerk, with the male customer unfortunately also within earshot.

"Do you have those white shoes in the window in size ten?" I asked. I tried to somehow make it seem mundane.

"Oh, those heels," said the clerk. "You like those, huh?"

He could have been a Dr. Seuss character. The Clerk With A Smirk. I knew I was busted, and the best answer to his question was none at all. I knew that in this case, any attempt to invoke a sister or girlfriend would fail miserably. Seconds of agonizing silence followed.

"Wellll...let me just see," he finally said, drawing out the words.

While he was in back, I felt as if I were on a pedestal for the other customers, wearing a pageant-style sash that said "Sissy."

Returning with a box, the clerk went for my jugular.

"And will you be trying these on, Sweetie?"

"No," I muttered, desperately wishing this could be seen as a big joke between us.

"Well would you be interested in a matching purse? We have some that would look really cute with those, you know."

He not only *knew,* our eye contact made it clear *he knew that I knew he knew.* I felt humiliation as never before, the kind I'd always known I might face someday. At this point I was finally allowed to pay and leave, and I told myself I could never try such a thing again.

But we CDs rebound marvelously from our setbacks. Upon reaching the mall corridor and spotting no one I recognized, my mood brightened considerably. Mortifying as it had been, it was over. I'd never see any of those people again, and I had the shoes! Those beautiful shiny high heels, fit for the sexiest girl you'd ever want to see. I allowed a fluttery sigh to run through me.

But what if they didn't fit? What a crushing blow that would be! I certainly would be incapable of returning them, and what if size ten in shoes like this was different from less sexy ones? Dangerous and unwieldy as it was, I had to try them on right there in the car in the crowded mall lot.

Hallelujah. It seemed they would fit. I was one happy girly boy on the drive home. Of course they would be difficult to walk in, but I was confident I could master them. I knew I would try as hard as I'd ever tried anything, and it wasn't as if I envisioned ever wearing them for any extended journey.

In another "first" from our eight years in Memphis, Valerie and I addressed my nature with a psychologist. And for the only time, I wound up subjecting myself to what I see in retrospect as an attempt at conversion therapy.

We hadn't sought out the therapist solely to tackle the CD issue. Valerie was not making a particular issue of it, and there were other areas in our relationship that we agreed could use some work. But, of course, my dressing came up.

"I presume you'd prefer this not be a part of your life and your relationship," said our counselor. She was a petite and short-haired woman, much older than us. She smoked almost nonstop.

"Well I guess so," I replied. "It's not like I beat myself up about it all the time, but I know it's problematic."

"I love him," Val said, "but I wish he didn't need to do it. It scares me that people might find out."

Our interlocutor nodded and offered a plan, suggesting I seek a meditative state in which I would associate being dressed with unpleasant occurrences. Perhaps, we all concurred, it could serve over time to diminish dressing's appeal. We tried it right there in her office.

"Close your eyes and imagine walking down a long stairway as you distance your mind from where you are now," she said. "Don't rush, but when you reach the bottom and your mind seems clear and relaxed, envision that you are wearing a dress."

"OK, I'm there," I said after perhaps five minutes.

"But this isn't a good thing," she said. "You don't really want to be like this. You feel ashamed."

"OK."

"And now you want to visualize. You have literally become covered in human excrement. It's all over that dress, and in your hair. Look at it and smell it. Is this what you want?"

Dutifully, I said no.

"Then imagine coming slowly back up the stairs, and as you come the shame and filth are subsiding. And now you open your eyes again and we're here. So how do you feel?"

"OK, I guess. Maybe that'll do something. I guess I can try it at home."

And I actually did. I imagined the shit again, and also feeling really nauseated. On the positive side, I imagined being straight and getting it on with a girl at the *Press-Scimitar* who I'd always thought was sexy.

Of course it was all bullshit in the end, and the end wasn't long in coming. I ditched it after about a week, and it was another week before Val even realized I had.

"That's OK. It seemed weird to me, too," she said. "I wasn't comfortable when you were doing it in her office."

And though psychologists have been quite helpful to Valerie and me through the years on a wide array of issues, we didn't return to this practitioner.

The failure of that venture served to emphasize that my urge to dress wasn't going anywhere. It was not long after when I mustered the nerve— or perhaps more accurately I just couldn't resist the urge—to take my show outside the house. At times when Valerie was gone, most often with those girlfriends, I took to getting as femme as I could, waiting until dark, and venturing out in the car.

These were my first times out en femme since that ill-conceived lipstick drive in tenth grade, and they were exhilarating.

*Here I am, world, deal with it.*

One time I perceived that some questionable-looking people were honking and attempting to follow me, but I took evasive action and they disappeared. Perhaps it was just my paranoia, but they hadn't seemed friendly.

The most exposure I could bear outside the vehicle was to park at our neighborhood bank branch and walk up to the outdoor ATM. I'd stand there a few moments, head on a swivel to make sure no other cars were entering the area, and I'd feign a transaction. Then it was quickly back to the car. If still no other cars were entering the area, maybe I'd do it again. Maybe I'd do it even a third time.

I knew that in a sense it was pathetic, but I had a visceral need to get my feminine side out, and almost every possible avenue came with potential life-altering consequences. The ATM trip was the best possible blend of exposure and safety, allowing me to walk around in a dress and heels, in a spot where I wouldn't be observed closely but might be seen and actually pass for a woman from afar.

Getting home from the ATM was no problem, until it was. About the third time I did this, I returned to see lights blazing all over our next-door neighbors' home. They clearly had guests, and the weather was temperate, so windows were open and doors were ajar. We were good friends with these neighbors, Larry and Mary, and it seemed just way too risky to attempt pulling into our driveway (we had no garage) and walking into the house. If Larry saw my car pull in, he'd come out, wanting me to join them.

Waiting for things to quiet down would not only be torturous, the delay would invite the likelihood of Valerie returning home. I was positive she had no inkling I was up to stuff like this. She would be shocked and perhaps tell me this stuff was going too far, so it was incumbent on me to save her the nasty surprise. I had to get in the house.

My only option as I saw it was to park two blocks up the street, take off my heels, and begin stealthily barefooting it. Our street was not a busy one, and I stayed close to shrubs and trees at the homes that seemed relatively darkened. When it was time to go past Larry's place, I held my breath, crossed to the other side of the street, and went past his house as quickly and quietly as I could. Then I stood close to the concealment of a friendly fir, making sure no one was wandering out of Larry's place, before taking the opportunity to recross to the safety of home.

Intense? No doubt. My heart was thudding as I hit the couch. Big fun? Kind of. No one was the wiser, and that was what mattered. But soon this sort of escapade would get noticeably tougher, because soon I would be a cross-dresser with a kid.

## CHAPTER 16

# PARENTHOOD

In January of 1978, just before buying our home in Memphis, Valerie and I sat in the living room of our small rental house and agreed it was time to start a family. We had been married five years. We were upbeat about our future, in the way one would hope all young couples could be.

But after trying for three years to conceive, with no success, we learned Valerie suffered from a fertility problem, endometriosis. We didn't become parents until January of '82, when the State of Tennessee granted our application for an adoption. We were twenty-nine, and after a qualification process that took only a few months, we were offered a four-month-old girl.

It was a Sunday night when our caseworker called. After a brief description of the situation regarding "Bonnie," who'd been given up for adoption by her unwed mother, we accepted without hesitation. We would pick her up directly from her foster family in Lebanon, Tennessee, some 240 miles east of Memphis.

We completed some paperwork at a Memphis state office on Monday morning and then headed east on I-40. Lebanon was just a bit beyond Nashville. We rolled up a long driveway to a pleasant rural home with plenty of acreage, and at my first sight of the bright-eyed and totally bald baby who would be ours, I was enraptured. It was agreed that we would take her back to our motel for a few hours, then return her to the foster folks and pick her up Tuesday morning for our return to Memphis.

The hours at our motel were magical. The tiny girl seemed quite happy with us, and we started calling her "Sarah," a name we had agreed on for our first female child while we were still in college. Despite our elation, we were happy enough to return Sarah to the foster home and enjoy one last night for just the two of us. But Tuesday morning was unexpectedly the pits.

"This just is killing us," Sarah's foster mom said as we walked in.

The family had been pleasant enough the previous evening, but now the couple and their two grown children were as morose a foursome as surely could be found in the Volunteer State. Beyond unwelcoming, they bordered on hostile.

"Bonnie belongs here," the mom said. "The state should have let us keep her. We thought they would. We told them how it would be best for Bonnie, how she is so happy here. But they said no. They wouldn't break the foster agreement. And now you're here to take her away from us."

Suddenly we were covillains with the state, and it was just them and us, in their house. I feared they might resist us physically. But we stood our ground, albeit shakily, and after a bit of silent treatment the family had Sarah's things ready to go.

"Can you at least give us fifteen minutes to say goodbye?" the dad asked. "You just don't seem to know or care what this is doing to us."

We agreed to wait in our car. It was a long quarter hour, marked by dark imaginings about a backdoor escape. I also thought of complaining to the state about how unfit these folks seemed to be in the foster parent role. But they answered our knock at the fifteen-minute mark, and we steeled our will to get Sarah to the car as quickly as possible. The sight of that house in rearview was a massive relief.

About sixty miles short of Memphis, we decided to stop for lunch. But lunch was suddenly a brand-new ballgame.

"Maybe we should just use the drive-through," Valerie said.

"No, I really want to go in," I said. Sitting down for a decent lunch was always a highlight for me on road trips. Up to this point, anyway.

"We can do this," I said. "We might as well start learning now."

"Nooooo!" Val yelled as I pulled Sarah from her car seat. "You can't just carry her in there! What are you gonna do when your food comes?"

"You mean I have to take this whole car seat thing in there? It's a pain in the ass to get unfastened."

"We can get one that's easier to use."

"How much will that cost us?"

I always fumed about such expenses imposed by life. She usually didn't.

"If you want to eat inside, she's got to be contained."

And so she was. Sarah was a bit crabby, and I looked around to see if anyone seemed annoyed, but no one did. People with kids of their own, I have learned, are often not much bothered by kids whose crabbiness is someone else's responsibility.

Most importantly, Valerie and I were in this together 100 percent, and we muddled through with love and good humor. We were meant for this, we both knew, and mostly it was great. Still, when Val commented on how nice it was that we didn't have to be so concerned with fertility considerations like taking her temperature to see when she was most fertile, I said, "You ought to keep taking your temperature, and the next time it tells us we absolutely *have* to screw, let's not."

CHAPTER 17

# THE BIG SHAVE

Things at work had been continuing to get better. In 1981, when George had to miss the first leg of his annual column-writing trip to the World Series, he sent me, as the baseball writer, to replace him. It was Dodgers vs. Yankees in the Bronx for two games—positively phantasmagoric for a scribe who had been mired so long in desk shifts and high school coverage.

My final step to full rehab came in 1982, just five weeks after we got Sarah, when George's prized tennis writer abruptly left for another job just before the US National Indoor Championships, a major pro event on the lean Memphis sports calendar. I bailed George out before the tourney even started, scooping the rival *Commercial Appeal* by nabbing John McEnroe for a long phone interview, and when play began, I logged a full week of fourteen-hour days, leaving Valerie with nearly all the Sarah-tending.

I got off George's shit list just in time, because on November 1, 1983, the *Press-Scimitar* joined *The Fort Worth Press* on the roster of failed afternoon papers. This crash didn't come out of the blue—the impending closing was announced weeks in advance—and again I was spared the stress of unemployment. Lapides by this point was willing to recommend me to the Scripps-Howard afternoon (gulp!) daily in Cincinnati. To give George his due, he seemed to truly care about how his departing staffers would fare. I was excited to make the move to *The Cincinnati Post.*

Though life in Cincinnati would eventually offer me greater freedom of expression in my dressing, the closet door didn't open immediately. My don't-ask-don't-tell (DADT) agreement with Valerie remained, not much changed from the 1975 original, and though her resistance was eroding, the process was geologically slow and not to be very evident for some years.

But since our last few years in Memphis and into the Cincy years, her habits had afforded me roughly one chance per year for a week or even ten days of intense dressing, albeit still in secret. These oases materialized when Valerie would pack up whatever kid or kids we had at the time and visit the family in Texas. Val never worked more than part-time outside the home, so it was natural for her to be able to go once a year when her career-driven husband could not.

My anticipation would begin building long before these annual opportunities arrived. Weeks out from Val's departure date, I'd start a "countdown clock" on an index card, showing the number of hours remaining until I'd have the house to myself. If Val was leaving July 1, for example, then around June 10 I'd write down the number 480—for the 480 hours (twenty days) I still had to wait. Then I'd put the card away and try not to look at it for a while. If I refrained from picking it up again for a week, I could write down a dramatic new total, all the way down near 300. What stunning progress, right before my eyes! But often I couldn't wait that long to check the card, so the entry after 150 might be only 130, and so on. By the time the big day finally arrived, I would have made twelve to fifteen entries. When the count hit below three digits, I'd be like a kid before Christmas. I'd be so jacked up I wouldn't sleep well the night before Val was to leave.

Bizarre? I knew it could seem so. Pathetic? Maybe. But that's how strong and bottled up the urge was. This was literally a once-a-year deal, perhaps more accurately Sissy's Mardi Gras than her Christmas.

Now if you had been Valerie back then—knowing what you knew about the eye shadow in New Orleans, the full confession in Euless, and my wanting to dress for Vic—you wouldn't have needed a private detective to tell you I'd be femming it up some in your absence. But remember what I said about "guileless," because that's what she is, and I don't believe my dressing entered her mind at all during her first couple of trips.

"What have you been up to the last few days?" she might ask on one of our near-daily phone calls.

"Oh, not really all that much," I'd say, standing in the kitchen in a bra, hose, and makeup.

I loved her to death, but I hated it when her calls caught me in the middle of my prep. I was always overhyped, anxious to complete my transformation without anything going dreadfully wrong, like a huge eye makeup smudge.

I'd silently scold myself while ignoring Valerie's briefing on family activities in Texas.

*You said you were going to call her before you started getting ready, but you forgot! No one to blame but yourself.*

The call would end, and I would resume worrying whether the new skirt would fit.

I was happy enough with Valerie never thinking about it. I guess I hoped she never would. But a year before our move to Cincy, my own carelessness led her to it.

"I found this in the laundry room," she said one evening. "I don't recognize it. I guess it must be yours?"

It was a bra.

This was just a few days after she'd made a return from Texas, and damn it, I had failed at the crucial task of getting every last CD item washed and put away. These were always such icky moments over the years, those times when I let my dressing cross into Valerie's world. Though she would not be in a rage about it, I still felt great shame to have the reality of it sitting out there in the open. It threatened my default state of feeling relatively good about my nature. I hated having to confront it in her presence.

"I'm sorry," I said. "I'm sorry I didn't get that put away."

"So did you get dressed up while I was gone?"

"Yes, I figured it would be a good time since I wouldn't bother you."

"Well, I'd really prefer you not, but I guess I can't stop you. Just please be careful and respect my space."

Then the DADT switch flipped on. We quit talking about it for the moment. But even guileless Valerie was not going to forget forever.

"I guess you're going to dress up?"

It was year four of the trips. My first time getting "the questions" before she left.

"Well, yeah, I thought I probably would," I said. An understatement of mammoth proportions, that.

"Are you going to be careful?"

"I'm always careful. I don't want people finding out any more than you do."

She still didn't realize, bless her, that I'd be dressing almost every day for the fortnight she'd be gone. When you have only 14 available out of 365, you can't afford to waste any. Nor did Val realize, or have a suspicious bone to wonder, whether I'd be leaving the house dressed. In my view, it didn't constitute lying to simply omit volunteering that this was becoming routine.

"Just make sure you clean up all your stuff before I get home," she'd say. "I shouldn't have to see any of that, and you're not always good about it."

*Deal. Done. Kiss-kiss, I really do love you. Have a great time in Texas. I'll miss you. Bye now.*

In early March of 1984, three months into our being Cincinnatians and a few weeks before one of Val's trips, I was struck by another of those CD urges, sudden and strong, that command bold action.

Could I possibly…might I actually…shave my legs?

What a huge step up that would be! If you're a CD out to look sexy, hairy legs showing under your hose is a big problem. It looks gross, at least to me, and I had been enduring this forever, ignoring it as best I could. Shaving was a dream that always seemed far too drastic, but as I got used to periodically having two weeks alone, the temptation grew stronger. And suddenly now, at age thirty-one, shaving was on the table for consideration.

Before the week was out, I knew I would do it. The prospect was simply too delicious to worry over aftershocks.

I figured that if I shaved the very first night, and not again, enough hair would grow back by the time Valerie got home that she might not notice. And if she did notice? Sorry, brain, we are just not going to think about that now. We are thinking about those cheerleaders we checked out at the University of Cincinnati basketball game the other night. We are thinking that before long, my legs are going to be as smooth and pretty as the wheels on those girls.

Talk about intoxicating. Talk about minutes seeming like hours as the big night approached.

But the act of shaving proved difficult and frustrating, because I really am in the ninetieth percentile for hairiness. In high school, I was among the very few who could grow a massive pair of mutton-chop sideburns, and I was quite proud of it. In the football or basketball locker room, my fuzzy chest and legs were a source of mild envy among the fellas. As an adult, I once won a "hairy chest" contest on a cruise ship.

But don't just take it from me; take it from the former Cincinnati Bengals fullback Jeff Cothran, via my longtime friend Geoff Hobson, a Bengals beat writer for *The Cincinnati Enquirer* at the time. Bengals players often saw me in states of undress during my twenty-four years with the club, as I regularly worked out and showered at the stadium.

"I'm just walking through the locker room," Hobson told me, "and Cothran is the only other guy in there; most of the players were already gone for the day. We're walking toward each other from opposite entrances, and suddenly we hear you getting paged on the intercom. And just as Cothran and I are passing close to each other, he looks up toward the ceiling and says, not really to anyone but himself, 'Jack Brennan…hairiest motherfucker I ever saw.'"

So my two disposable twin-blade razors were overmatched on that first-ever leg-shaving night. I guess I had not seen it as all that different from shaving my beard, but the sheer volume of hair and the amount of skin to smooth up soon had me in a razor-mucking and drain-clogging mess. I didn't give up—I positively refused to give up—but it took at least two hours. Reaching all those nooks and crannies on your knees and ankles and whatever, without cutting yourself, is the stuff of intermediate-level yoga.

And once I finally got it done, I had to face the reality that I was missing a key element to enjoying it: smoking pot. I had been a regular pot smoker since college, but at this early stage of Cincinnati life I had not yet found a consistent local dealer.

Since the fine pleasure of getting stoned while admiring my shaved legs was not going to happen, I made do as best I could with some beer. Once shaved, I spent time on regular sissy activities, including trips out to an ATM or uncrowded shopping-center parking lot.

It hadn't been everything I had hoped it would be, this leg-shaving, but after twenty-plus years of hairy legs, that smooth skin was a galvanizing experience. I was resigned to facing any consequences. But potential peril popped up sooner than expected. I would have to navigate a different and dicey situation before Valerie's return from Texas.

The basketball team from Cincinnati's Xavier University was advancing in the National Invitation Tournament, a big deal for the XU program at that time, and on short notice the *Post* assigned me to assist Bill Koch, then the Xavier beat writer, at a third-round game at the University of Michigan. My addition to the trip would be easy on the budget, as Bill was driving to Ann Arbor. We could ride together and...we would also share a hotel room.

Bill knew as well as Jeff Cothran what a hairy motherfucker I was. We had often played pickup basketball and tennis together. I knew I'd have to hide my shaved gams while changing or lounging in our room, and I worried that Bill would notice how modest I was, always exiting the john in sweatpants and getting into same right out of bed. I didn't curse myself for shaving, but I cursed cruel fate for letting this come up so shortly after.

As it turned out, Bill appeared to pay no attention whatsoever. But I had endured several days of stress. And still there was Valerie to deal with.

I confessed immediately upon her return from Texas. I could say that I knew I owed her that, but what I knew even better was that my hair had not grown back as I'd hoped. Not even close, as vast fields of stubble still covered my legs. This could not be long hidden, and surprise self-discovery by Valerie was not recommended. The forthright approach, painful as it would be, was the preferred horn of the dilemma.

"Shaving your legs? You didn't tell me you were going to do anything like that!"

She was mad. I had no comeback. I mumbled weakly about a "spur of the moment" decision. I braced immediately for further brickbats, but the biggest one didn't land until bedtime.

"You're all prickly! It itches. Move over! I like your hair, and I like it when it's long and soft."

She sharply limited contact in bed for a week or more. Still, I didn't regret shaving. Those hairless legs had just felt so good. Valerie chose within a reasonable time to remove this from our cause célèbre list, and I noted to myself that while she clearly had said she didn't want me to shave again, I had not been asked to swear a blood oath to a lifetime ban.

# THE CD LIFE:
# TAN OPAQUE HOSE

"Shelley" was a strange downer of a CD who gave me the single best transformation tip of my dressing career. I'll always remember him fondly for it, even though he was no fun at all as a bar companion.

I met Shelley on one of my infrequent visits to cross-dresser support meetings in the late nineties. We went out together once, which was approved by both Val and our therapist at the time, and I learned he was negative and cynical about everything. He never became the gal pal I had hoped for, but before he departed my life, Shelley left me with the indispensable secret of *tan opaque hose*. Shaving my legs was still taboo, fifteen years after Valerie had blasted me for doing it when she was in Texas, and I had gone out with Shelley looking the same lame way I always did—with very hairy legs encased incongruously in sheer hose. I had always disdained tights as too thick and unsexy, so the hair-and-hose look was an unfortunate staple.

But Shelley clued me in that the right kind of opaque hose—medium tan and not too thick—did a marvelous job of hiding hair and mimicking a shaved leg. Just slip a pair of sheer hose over the opaque, Shelley said, and you are ready to rock and roll.

He was right. I could barely believe how good and femme-shaved my legs looked with Shelley's two-step plan. It was the biggest instant upgrade in my CD history, boosting my confidence when out in the world for years to come.

So thanks again, Shelley, and I hope your life has gotten a little more positive.

## CHAPTER 18

# A CD HALLOWEEN

While my cross-dressing was still awaiting its eventual Cincinnati blossoming, my sports-fan side loved our new city instantly. The Queen City was the original US pro sports town, widely accorded that status for the 1869 baseball Reds, the first club to pay all its players. I aspired to cover games of the Reds and the NFL Bengals in my job at *The Cincinnati Post*, and even if I never did, life as a sports enthusiast just figured to be so much more interesting than in Memphis.

Cincinnati also promised a new cultural vibe for a guy from Texas and then Tennessee, and I had zero qualms about becoming a Yankee. I had always rather aspired to Yankeedom, in fact. My Texas roots were shallow—my folks being job-related transplants from St. Louis—and I never bought into Texas braggadocio or cowboy culture. Nor did I have any taste for the South's incredibly wide load of conservative bullshit, even if the Memphis brand was perhaps not so bad as the Deep South. Though Cincinnati lies but barely out of the South, with suburbs across the Ohio River in Kentucky, it was definitely "the North" to Valerie and me.

My sports editor at the *Post*, Doug Henry, was karma payback for my early Memphis years with George Lapides. When the pro-football beat writer job came open just four months into my time on staff, Doug told me I was his boy for the Bengals.

For the first time in nine years, since the day the *Fort Worth Press* died, my career was on a proper track. I was assigned to the Bengals on a daily basis, including travel to all road games, and in this era, most newspapers sent their major league beat writers to the league playoffs even when the home team didn't qualify. To close the 1984 NFL season, I spent a week in San Francisco among the journalism herd covering Super Bowl XIX between the 49ers and Miami Dolphins. To call it a blast would be a considerable understatement.

The following football season, the *Post* featured my photo on a "rack card," a promotional insert on the self-service sales boxes that were located all over town. The cards read, "Jack Brennan covers the Bengals, because the *Post* means sports," and I imagined a tag line underneath that read: "Bleep you, Lapides."

After six months in the apartment where I did The Big Shave, Valerie and I found a great home in the city area called Oakley, with many neighbors about our age. We came to call our little area "The Cove" due to the cul-de-sac several of our homes fronted. We saw one another almost daily, partied when the mood struck (often), and watched out for each other's property and kids.

Most of The Cove's guys played basketball regularly. I was among the founding core of "Coveball," which employed a portable hoop in the cul-de-sac, with a free-throw lane and three-point arc painted in the street. (A cop yelled at us about that once, but nothing ever came of it.) Beyond immediate neighbors, the games regularly attracted five or six of my newspaper friends and some pals of other neighbors as well. I talked a lot of sports, and everyone thought it was cool that I covered the Bengals.

More marvelously, Valerie and I were able to get pregnant. Twice. We had launched plans for a second adoption in '86, but Val meanwhile found a gynecologist, Stewart Friedman, who treated her endometriosis, allowing her to get pregnant. Tim was born in June of '87 and Hannah in May of '89, and Sarah was a superb big sister. We loved being the parents of three. Valerie was the primary caretaker, but I think I ran up good fatherhood scores every year.

As for dressing, it was slowly becoming more normalized. I still had to keep it on the down-low, indulging only when Val was away from the house, but it wasn't a major incident if I left a pair of heels on the floor in the basement. And in the fall of '87, between Tim's and Hannah's births, I was presented with a glorious new opportunity. As Halloween approached and Cove party plans were being laid, my excellent friend and next-door neighbor Dave Johnson suggested that the guys dress as women. Just as a lark, you know? I could never have been so bold as to propose such a thing—I would never have even dreamed it—but with cover from Dave, of course I was all in.

"Do you really have to?"

That was the strongest objection Valerie mustered for this one. It hadn't been my idea, and all the guys were going to do it. The other wives—from a different perspective than Val's, admittedly—seemed to think it would be a hoot.

I didn't do a countdown clock for this opportunity, but I developed an obsession with weather forecasts. Halloween in Cincinnati can be beautiful one year and crappy cold the next, so I was praying it would be nice enough to allow our customary outside partying without the need for heavy coats.

Bingo. Conditions were warm enough for me to present in a springlike dress. Though it was clearly just a big joke for the other guys, I was committed to testing the slippery slope between kidding around and enjoying the experience too transparently.

"You're wearing mascara?" Valerie challenged as I dolled up. Yes I was, and I was also wearing lipstick and hose and some low heels. I couldn't shave my legs—that was still on Valerie's bridge-too-far list—and besides, it would have exposed me too baldly to the neighbors. But I wasn't holding back in any other respect. It was just a Halloween costume, right?

I've always wondered how much the neighbors noticed my enthusiasm.

"Oh, aren't you lookin' hot tonight!" someone said, and that felt great. But nobody tried to engage me on the extent of my preparations, and it was just such complete fun to be having an adult social time, getting a little loose, while presenting as a girl. Not that I minced around or otherwise acted "too queer," but this was a case of being accepted in a dress that was far more exciting than the "Angela Angleworm" high school play or my visit with Cousin Vic. I'd dash into the house frequently to check and possibly improve my look. Or maybe I just desired the mirror to confirm this was really happening. I wouldn't have wanted to be doing anything else, anywhere, that night.

As the evening wore down, after the other guys had tired of their womanhood, I was still fully dressed, chatting with a single lady, a nurse named Pamela, on her porch. Whatever we were talking about didn't matter; this just seemed the best spot for me to extend my experience. But Pamela clearly had an inkling of my true motivation and a mind to keep me from sliding too far down that slope.

"I guess this costume deal is about over," she observed. "Maybe it's time for you to wind it down, too?"

Pamela deftly maintained plausible deniability regarding any inference that I was a true CD. She didn't press me to acknowledge something I wasn't ready for at that time. I wouldn't officially be "out" to her as neighborhood life moved on. But I appreciated her kind intentions and reluctantly took her up on the suggestion. And when November 1 dawned, if any of the other neighbors were gossiping about me, I didn't sense it.

But thirty-two years since that blouse swap with Janie, I was fully out to only two people—Valerie and Vic—and feelings that were totally natural to me could not be expressed to anyone. Not my attraction to a cute dress in a store window, not my comments about the products in cosmetics ads, and not my desire to someday play tennis with smooth, shaved legs. Val didn't want to hear it, Vic lived a thousand miles away, and it seemed there was just no path to escaping a life marked by secrecy and fear of exposure. I could randomly select fifteen people in my life—hell, make it thirty or even a hundred—and the chance of my ever coming out to any seemed the same across the board: zero.

It all felt a little worse than usual after the Halloween festivities. Parading in a skirt with regular straight friends had just been such fun, yet there was no prospect of such a thing ever happening again. Maybe, I thought, it would have been better to have passed on that intense but all too brief experience, because now I knew what I was missing.

I figured I'd probably finish my time on earth with all but Valerie and Vic walled off from my full humanity. Until, that is, the serendipitous nature of life served to unexpectedly double the number of those in the know.

## CHAPTER 19

# PAM AND I

It was around May of 1988 when my CD world expanded again. The first to join Valerie and Vic was Pam Johnson—not the Pamela who had advised me to ditch my dress on Halloween, but rather the wife of Dave, the next-door neighbor who had suggested drag for Halloween.

We tended to party late in The Cove, and this night found Pam and me in a third neighbor's backyard approaching 2:00 a.m., after everyone else had crashed. Pam is a very sweet and talkative person, an open-book personality, and before long, she was spouting to me about some very personal details in her life. As she bared her soul, I began thinking, *If Pam can go on at such length with me about her personal stuff, why can't I tell her about mine?*

So I did. It took about fifteen minutes to muster the courage. I was so self-absorbed that I barely comprehended whatever Pam was saying during that time.

"You know," I finally said, "there's something personal I want to share, too. Remember Halloween, when all the guys dressed up as girls? That wasn't just a one-night deal for me. I've had the urge to do that ever since I was a little kid, and I still do it, but you're only the third person to know. Val and a male cousin of hers, who's gay, are the only other two."

"Wow. I never would have guessed that in a million years," she said. "You're so much...well, I don't know, just one of the guys. That is really a trip! But it's cool. Do you ever go out to clubs or anything?"

Now my gears were whirring furiously, heart pounding.

"I never have," I said. "I'd be too uptight to do it by myself. But I think it would be really fun. Do you think we could ever go out together...as girlfriends, I mean?"

"Hell, yeah," came the response. "I think that would be a fucking blast."

There was no "Well, let me think about it." No "Maybe, but I'll have to ask Dave." I instantly knew this was going to happen, unless one of us died or something.

But as often occurs with flashes of inspiration about marvelous CD adventures, a real-life obstacle reared its head: Dave would have to be clued in as well. I knew it would be a very bad deal for Pam and me to attempt this on the sly. Val of course would have to be informed as well, but I figured she wouldn't balk too badly with Pam involved. But Dave? No one knew a thing about me among straight male buddies.

"But there's a first time for everything," I quickly told myself. This prize of an opportunity was far too precious to pass up. And I knew I wouldn't have to find the guts to tell Dave myself. Pam would do it for me.

"He won't care," she said. "Don't worry about it."

I did, of course, but two days later Pam said, "I told him. He's fine with it."

I still had the yips about seeing Dave for the first time after the tell. But when that happened, incredibly to me, our friendship changed not an iota. We kept on talking sports and playing hoops and going to ballgames and drinking beer. He never offered even a hint about what Pam and I had planned until the day before, and it was only to wish us a good time. Perhaps I should have pondered this more fully in regard to possible openings to other friends, but I was focused only on this huge night out.

Valerie was on a Texas trip while all of this played out, and it was after the fact when I fessed up to her. She frowned, but she didn't go ballistic. By this time, she knew I'd be up to something while she was gone, and she was beginning to achieve a comfort level with people knowing about me as long as they were trusted friends.

"Really," she said, predictably, "I guess I'd rather you did it with Pam than by yourself."

"You look great!" Pam had said to me when we met to start our evening. "You look really sexy."

The compliment couldn't have been more welcome, because for the occasion I had found a super-hot shiny pink pleated skirt at Kohl's. It was a wrap-around that buttoned all the way down the front. The buttons were adorable.

Hot damn. We were two seductive chicks, and this was to be my first time inside a public building en femme, the first time out of the house when I did not self-limit to parking lots or obscure areas of shopping centers. I was going to show myself to some people, maybe even interact a bit.

I still hadn't adopted a confirmed femme name at this point. "Jackie" was an obvious candidate, but it didn't sit completely well that my family had called me that as a small child. It felt like a boy's name—or even a man's, a la Jackie Gleason—so part of me kept searching for something sounding more purely feminine. Also, "Jackie" was perhaps too perilously close to "Jack." This question was not to be decided for a number of years, but for this night with Pam, I decided to be "Lisa." It just sounded girly.

All our plans were my ideas. Pam was just along for wherever the ride took us. We headed for The Dock, a big gay club that was, characteristically, in rather an armpit neighborhood on the western edge of Cincinnati's downtown. I'd never been there—I'd never been to any gay club—but The Dock was the "big box" gay club in Cincinnati, almost an Ikea among lesser-known hideaways scattered Lord-knew-where.

For sure I could not have handled going dressed to a mainstream establishment at this point. The prospect of disapproval from Straight America was too fearsome. Wouldn't everyone deride me as a pathetic pansy? Wouldn't there be at least a chance someone from the Bengals or a media acquaintance would be there?

The Dock would be plenty scary for me.

Big-box as it may have been, The Dock held to what seems a maxim for Midwestern queer bars: the unwritten rule that "All establishments must have exteriors that have no clear signage and look unwelcoming." It was in a prefab metal building that formerly served some industrial purpose. Its neighbors included a power station, a homeless camp under a highway overpass, and a couple of trash-strewn fields. The entrance was windowless and badly in need of some comforting neon. One "Bud Light" sign would have made a world of difference. The front door was olive drab and latched in a fashion that looked difficult to operate.

"Are you sure this place is even open?" Pam asked.

I noted the presence of other cars in the parking lot and determined that bold action was called for. By her.

"You go in first, if you can get the door open," I suggested. "You won't draw as much attention as I would."

My brave girlfriend did it—the door was actually a snap—and our eyes beheld the scene: a large bar with thirty to forty people in it. Who knew?

There would be a band, and a relatively friendly person accepted our cover charges. We checked out the scene, and some in the scene checked us out, but cursorily at best. I imagined cross-dressers were not a rarity at this venue, though I didn't spot any others this night, and the two of us were just like any other two friends at a bar. We had some drinks, we talked, and we had some limited interaction with other patrons. Maybe 35 percent were obviously queer, maybe 10 percent pretty surely straight, and the rest you just couldn't tell.

Twenty minutes in, I craved more excitement. It was all about the buzz, right? After another fifteen minutes of obsessing on a single thought, I became brave enough to broach it to Pam.

"Hey, do you think you could get a guy to dance with me? I'm too shy to ask myself, but it would be fun. Just to flirt a little, I mean, no heavy body contact or anything."

This night was all about me, and she said she'd give it a try. I shivered as I saw her canvassing other tables. What would I feel if a man were actually in my personal space, asking me to be his dance partner? Then Pam was headed back my way.

"I tried my best," she said, "but nobody seemed to want to."

I had to just accept it. It had been a big ask, I knew.

I went out with Pam a few more times during this late-eighties period, not hiding it from Valerie but still doing it only when she was in Texas. Pam and I once just hung out at my place, and after a few beers, as we sat on the deck, she asked, "When you're dressed like this, would you rather have sex with a man or a woman?"

"Dressed like this," I replied, "I think it would be a man."

This led me to show her a magazine depicting cross-dressers engaging in sex with men. This in turn led me to show her a couple of my dildos. I had no illusion that I'd ever act on these fantasies, and I told Pam that, insisting I'd never be unfaithful to Valerie. Pam remained simply the supportive friend. "Do whatever makes you happiest," she suggested.

I didn't relate that conversation to Valerie. Though I hadn't tried to hide that Pam and I would meet occasionally, Val and I remained in DADT mode about most details of those meetings.

In summer of 1989, I would find circumstances right for another coming out, one that would lead me to sometimes take my dressing on the road.

## CHAPTER 20

# A DEATH IN THE FAMILY

My next breakthroughs in coming out arose from a family tragedy.

In June of 1988, Valerie's brother Brian, six years her elder at forty-two, died of a heart attack in his suburban Dallas home. His cremation and funeral took place in Waco, where Val's parents had relocated a few years earlier, but there was no immediate burial. The family was undecided regarding the disposition of his ashes, and it was not until a year later that a plan was set for burial in a family plot in Waco. So in July of '89, we were back in Central Texas, and with a year passed since everyone's most intense grief, I sensed a chance.

Diane, Brian's widow and Valerie's unofficial big sister, could become the fifth person to know of me.

Diane was quite the free spirit. She had been close to genuine hippie status in the late '60s—at least that was my impression—and not long after Val and I graduated high school, she and Brian had given us our first taste of pot. She was forty-one when Brian died and still very into a counterculture lifestyle.

Brian and Diane had always seemed a bit of an odd couple. They both liked to party for sure, but Brian was much more conservative. He had spent his boyhood in Waco, a Baptist stronghold even by Texas standards, and his only postsecondary schooling had been a year as a military cadet at the very conservative Texas A&M University. His jobs had been blue-collar, and he leaned further right than his parents. It seemed Diane was always tugging Brian toward the liberal side, but never with full success.

When I first met Brian, I was just seventeen to his full-fledged adult of twenty-three, and I was intimidated by his Texas hard-ass side.

"Brian bullied me when I was little," Valerie had told me early on. "He was the first kid and I was the second, and I felt like he didn't want me around. Diane has helped him, though, just with emotional growth, and we've gotten along much better the last few years. But he still can't totally give up that Texas tough-guy image."

I learned just not to mention some things around Brian. He had drilled that into me when I let it slip that Val and were I going to a flower show.

"Sounds like a good place to find a bunch of pussies," he said. "Take Diane if you want. Me and Jim are workin' on his car today."

Or maybe he'd be going hunting.

"You ever bag a five-point buck?" he might ask. "I guess not. You ever even fired a shotgun before? Are you sure you were born in Texas?"

I'm not saying we were enemies. His kidding was generally good-natured, and he honored my place in Valerie's life. He seemed, however, to be one of the very last acquaintances to whom I'd ever come out.

But now Brian was gone, and on this trip a full year after his death, it dawned effortlessly that there was nothing so scary now about opening up to Diane.

It figured to be easy to grab a private moment with her on the Wednesday evening before she was to return to Dallas from the burial. I just needed to be ready when she made her evening visit to a large county park across the street from Val's parents' home. Diane and I were both patrons of the park, as the area offered convenient getaways (including the chance for a few tokes) from the loving but bacchanal-free zone of the family compound.

When I saw her go, I waited a few minutes to make sure nobody else needed me, and I followed. I briefly despaired that I wouldn't find her. It was getting dark, and it really is a big park. But eventually I spotted her beyond some trees leading down to Lake Waco. I was nervous to the point of distraction, but my urge to come out was far stronger than my fear of rejection.

I took a pass on pleasantries of the "lake sure is pretty tonight" variety. I just blurted it all out, and Diane was more than receptive.

"I think that is really cool," she said, "and it's also very cool that you're sharing it with me. Sometimes I feel like the only strange one in this family. I mean I've known you were a liberal, but still you seemed pretty straight like the rest of them. I am really happy to have some company. I'd love to talk more sometime about your feelings."

Oh, I had a plan for that. Since Valerie desired a few more days with her folks, I could go to Dallas on Friday and have a sissy night with Diane. I'd return to Waco on Saturday, and Sunday we'd be heading back to Cincinnati.

Valerie accepted it. This was another CD reveal involving a close and trusted person in our world, and particularly so in Valerie's. She wasn't going to resist if my destination was Diane's. And it was easy enough to explain to the rest of the family that Jack and Diane would enjoy a little "in-laws time" together. Everyone seemed to agree that would be nice.

Sadly, this remarkable opportunity had arrived with all my girl stuff a thousand miles away in Cincinnati. I would be sorely lacking some essentials for the full dressing, hair, and makeup experience that I craved. Shopping opportunities would be limited. But perfect would not be allowed to be the enemy of good.

The day I left for Dallas, I drove the two hours as early as I could politely get away. Then I rushed with uncharacteristic incautiousness through as much shopping as I could. I bought a skirt and blouse, a bra, some makeup, and pantyhose. I also bought a women's hat to cover my manly hair.

I was thirty-six, an established sportswriter in Cincinnati, ready for my fifth straight year as a pro-football beat writer. I had been married fifteen years and had just been blessed with my third kid. I was as straight as could be to 99 percent of those who knew me. Those concepts crossed my mind during that rush shopping job in Dallas. But in the end, there was nothing to do but shrug, chuckle, and move on. An exciting night lay ahead.

CHAPTER 21

# DOING DALLAS

Though Brian and Diane's family home was in a conventional Dallas suburb, Diane for several years had leased an apartment in that same Dallas "gay area" where Valerie and I had first lived. She sought an environment that properly nurtured her artistic and bohemian sensitivities. It had been no secret to Brian or their three kids, and it was of course the perfect adults-only venue for my visit.

Despite our premise to the family in Waco, we didn't really visit much. Diane wasn't even around for most of the evening. She had plans, made prior to my big reveal, and she told me not to expect her until late. That was fine, since dressing had almost always been a solitary endeavor, and I enjoyed the feel of being in a new place. I ventured out only briefly, fearing I'd be easy to spot as male even from a distance, given my rushed-together outfit with no wig or heels.

Diane showed up around eleven o'clock and was ready to play the girlfriend role. It was so comfortable to be "out" with her, just like it had been with Pam. She had a sense for my wanting to share inner feelings and naughty desires, and she was willing to gently lead me on.

"So does it feel good to you to be a woman?"

"I don't want to be a woman all the time," I said, "but it does turn me on when I do it."

"What's it like being around a football team all the time, feeling the way you do?"

"I worry about people finding out—it would be extra humiliating in that environment—but I just don't give off any hints. I'm sure no one suspects a thing."

"Do you like to look at the players...in the locker room, I mean?"

"No," I said. "It's a workplace. I'm thinking about work when I'm in there."

It was a quiet night overall, and in the morning I was driving back to Waco, my girl stuff tightly packed. But the quality of the evening, per se, was less important than my growing realization that this could happen again, and in a better way. Subsequent Texas visits could offer more chances at Diane's, and with time to plan, I could have a full load of accessories brought from home.

Football played a key role in that next chance. In October 1991 I was headed for Dallas solo to cover a Bengals road game against the Cowboys for *The Cincinnati Enquirer,* where I had relocated after six years at the *Post.* On the Saturday night before the game, I would go to Diane's apartment, get settled in, and get pretty. Under cover of night, I'd go to a nearby queer club Diane had mentioned.

I brought a white rayon dress, all shiny. I had bought it a few years before, in San Diego, during a weeklong assignment covering the Super Bowl. Getting back into my hotel with my prize had been daunting, as I feared someone would see me and get curious about the JCPenney bag I was carrying, but I had managed to slip through without incident.

The Dallas club Diane had suggested was packed and boisterous, easy to enter without attracting much notice. A DJ type was working the crowd in a somewhat provocative way, and I was content just to watch and listen. But suddenly, the DJ was pointing to me.

"Hey, Sweetie over there," he assertively asked into his mic, "do you prefer to penetrate or to be penetrated?"

Oh, jeez. Now I stood out, even in this crowded place, the only CD in the room, and I was on the spot in an unprecedented way. I so wanted to say "be penetrated," but it was more than I could handle. I was still at a very tender stage of dressing in public, and my circuits overloaded. I froze.

A spotlight of some kind was on me, teaching me how it really feels to be a deer in the headlights.

I said not a word. I wanted only to escape.

"Speak up, there, Sweetie," the DJ said. "You're here, you're lookin' hot, and these people all want to know about you."

Still I was silent. Some catcalls began. And finally the DJ gave up and sought a new target. But I was soundly shaken, feeling that the whole place was still staring at me, and after about ten minutes of trying to chill, I decided I had to leave.

It was nice to be safely back at the apartment, until it got boring. I started second-guessing myself. Had it really been necessary to flee? Wouldn't I enjoy exiting the apartment again, driving back to the bar, and getting back into that mix? I couldn't help wishing the DJ would ask me that question again. I'd do better this time.

"Well, my weenie's pretty tiny and kinda soft," I'd say in character, blushing sweetly and batting my made-up lashes. "I can't penetrate, really. So I prefer to be penetrated."

Wouldn't that be just such a turn-on in front of a bunch of people?

So back I went, but I was out of luck. The DJ was gone, and the scene was not much different from a random bar in Cincinnati. After about twenty minutes of sitting mostly unnoticed, I realized it was after 1:00 a.m. And I had a damn Bengals game to cover the next day.

But late as it was upon reaching the apartment, I would not be turning in right away. Diane was there.

"Have fun?" she asked, and then I gave her a full report.

"Oh what a hoot!" she said. "You shouldn't have been so scared. But hey, you hadn't told me about wanting to 'be penetrated.' Have you ever tried it?"

"Not with anybody, of course," I said, "but I do have a dildo. I brought it with me."

I showed it to her.

"Well, are you gonna use it?"

"I guess I will," I said. "It hurts a little sometimes, but I like the feeling it leaves, of being just a little sore as a reminder after it's over."

"Well I'm going to bed," she said. "But you have a good time with your boyfriend!"

With that, and with deconstructing my female self and doing all my packing, it was three thirty before I hit the pillow. I needed to be checked in and fully set up at the Cowboys' stadium in suburban Irving no later than eleven, an hour before the noon kickoff. I managed that, but not long after settling in my seat, the chill of that first lipstick day at Cistercian Prep School was suddenly upon me again.

"Does your eye feel OK?" a writer friend was asking. "It looks like there's some kind of gunk or something in your left one."

"Gee, I don't know," I said, but of course I knew right away. I was in a football press box wearing mascara that hadn't been fully scrubbed, and I could only hope that at this point, it looked like something other than makeup.

But it did look like makeup to me, and the press box john was not the ideal spot to remedy the situation. It was crowded, like it always is in the minutes prior to kickoff, and it wasn't a place where guys were normally washing their faces. I had to wait for an uncrowded moment to get clean, and I missed kickoff before I got back to my seat. I was relieved, though, that my colleague had alerted me to the situation. I wouldn't have wanted to be in makeup three hours later when I went to the locker room to interview players and coaches.

It was one unpleasant grind of a day. I was operating on five hours' sleep, but it was worth enduring for the previous night's adventures. And my life on the road—reporting by day, dressing up by night—was just starting to kick into high gear.

# THE CD LIFE: NAILS

Every item in a CD's toolbox has its charms, but none can match the curious mix of pleasure, pain, and circumscription one gets from long artificial fingernails. I like my nails a good inch longer than my fingertips, well beyond what might be considered practical.

Nails don't require a mirror for self-admiration. They flash before the eye with every hand motion, and the huge array of polish colors keeps each experience fresh. But for your first few times in nails, unless they are really short, you might as well be wearing boxing gloves. It's nearly impossible to button a button, pry off a lid, lift a credit card off a flat surface, or even open a bag of chips. Writing with pen or pencil is a challenge, and forget operating a keyboard.

But it's a most distinctive feeling to be so constrained by your sexy nails. It reinforces your fantasy notion of being rather a china doll. A woman writing in *T: The New York Times Style Magazine* once made that point, saying she liked something about the feminine conditions that long nails impose. There's an erotic statement in nails, she wrote, precisely because of the ways they limit you and force you to adjust.

And, if I might add, they just look so damn hot.

I get that sexy-constrained feeling from my nails when I'm out en femme and need to use either a parking meter or gas pump. I know, from bitter experience, that if I slide my credit card into the reader on either device, the card will go in so far that I'll be unable to pull it back out. I'll be able to get only my nail tips onto the plastic, and those tips have zero pulling power. I've gotten stuck once each at a pump and a meter, and in each case, I mildly freaked out before realizing that I'd just have to ask someone's help.

The experience wasn't really so awful. Help was available each time, and it was sweet to have been a damsel in distress.

If you stay with it, you get a lot better at managing life in nails. You feel a sense of girly pride when you realize you are handling formerly difficult tasks without even thinking of your nails. One night when a surprise Bengals development caught me with my nails already on, I clickety-clacked the necessary news release from home on my laptop. It wasn't easy or fast, but I got a kick out of the experience. I recalled images of female office workers who typed just fine in long nails. Then I moved on with the rest of my night, feeling all the better at how I had functioned with those talons on.

I usually polish my press-on nails the night before I plan to wear them. I create ten double-sided pieces of duct tape, affix them to the back of a magazine and then secure a nail on each. This allows me to stroke the polish on aggressively, with no worry about mistakes, and the nails are nicely dry by the time I put them on. I love rich, red nails, of course, but also many other colors. Outlandish neon shades in yellow, orange, or lime green are tremendous on occasion. I've received numerous compliments from girls on my nails. They often seem to really think I've had them done at a salon. How fun!

## CHAPTER 22

# DRESSING ON THE ROAD

As I sat in the Cowboys' press box after my night at Diane's, it dawned that I didn't need special circumstances to make dressing on the road practicable. It didn't have to happen only in Dallas, and I didn't need a crash pad like Diane's apartment. I could do it on any Bengals trip, as long as I was up for the trouble required.

And like a true sissy, I was willing. Willing to pack all my girl stuff onto a plane with all my regular clothes and all my reporter's equipment. Willing to check baggage for trips of short duration. When Cincinnati media buddies were on the same flight, it could get awkward.

"What's in those bags?" someone might ask. "What could you possibly need on a trip like this that won't fit in a carry-on?"

"I guess I'm just not good at traveling light."

Lame as that sounded, I could never think of a better response.

I'd be carrying a dress, or a skirt and a blouse, and a bra, panties, and likely a slip. A bag full of makeup. Some jewelry. A wig. I liked dressy, sexy clothes, the kind a woman would wear on a big date with a man. My go-to shoes at this time were black patent-leather stiletto pumps, with about four-inch heels. I also loved black hose. So suggestive.

The freedom of sportswriter travel was an enabling factor in my escapades. Newspaper guys traveled as lone wolves, so I could usually build some dressing time into my itinerary. Scribes covering the Bengals would spend at least two nights in a road city, and we could arrive nice and early the Saturday before the game. "Arrival Saturdays" were particularly wide open when you worked for *The Cincinnati Post*, which had no Sunday edition—and, of course, there was no website in that era. So Saturday was always a pure "travel day." The Bengals could have cured cancer on a Saturday, and still I couldn't have reached *Post* readers about it until Monday afternoon.

On the first few trips, I just dressed and enjoyed it in the room. Staying in the room gets old, however. The urge to get out grows strong. At first, the best I could do was to timidly open my door, look to see if the coast was clear, and then do some walking up and down the corridor. Sounds lame again—I know—but strolling those halls all dolled up was exhilarating to me.

In January 1987, I was in Cleveland for an NFL playoff game that didn't involve the Bengals, so I could choose any hotel with a half-decent rate, and I booked the Airport Marriott because I knew it had first-floor rooms on hallways exiting straight into the parking lot. I didn't have to fret the presence of a Bengals traveling party, so finally I could *leave the hotel.*

I had fun with my usual activities, exiting the car in a couple shopping areas for brief strolls. Simply being out in a strange town was excitement enough in itself. But when I returned to the hotel, with perhaps a hundred feet of corridor to go before my door, my path was suddenly crossed by a group of young partiers bursting out of a room. I was caught dead to rights, in that same white dress I had worn in Dallas, and I had zero aplomb, only fright.

"Oh, look!" said a guy, with a mixture of a sneer and a giggle. "What in the world do we have here?"

"It's a verr-ee prett-ee girl," said another guy.

"Omigod, he's got on fucking high heels!" said a girl.

It was mortifying. The thirty seconds to reach my room and key myself inside seemed like thirty minutes.

The hooting didn't immediately abate, and I remained thoroughly freaked. Were these people going to start banging on my door? Demanding I come out or let them in? Might I get beaten up?

Though it was only about eight o'clock, it seemed imperative to end my sissy evening: scrub off the makeup, peel down the hose, put the dress and heels away.

But during that process, my fear began to subside, and I questioned the necessity of shutting down. It had been quiet now for some time, and hadn't the experience seemed girly as all get out despite the big scare? And I so wanted to continue being a girl for the evening.

I redid my makeup and whatever else I had taken down, and the evening got back on track. It was a hassle to have to get dressed again, but the attraction of it was doubled in a sense. I was bound to my sissy nature; I *had* to redo it. That feeling was part of the fantasy fun as well.

While I had been genuinely scared, I still wanted people to notice. Otherwise, what's the point? The trick is getting noticed in a way that works for you, a way that doesn't threaten you emotionally.

During Super Bowl week in Miami after the 1988 season, I got way more notice than I had banked on. The Bengals were in the game, making my workload considerable, but I still found the time to dress. As we say in sports, I was motivated.

On the Monday after the Sunday game, I found that I could stay an extra night at the hotel as long as I filed a fresh follow-up story for Tuesday. I called the hotel desk first thing Monday to extend my reservation, and then I thought, *What the hell, let's write the story en femme*. It was always fun to extend dressing into an otherwise "normal" task or activity.

After eating and fixing myself up, I was ready about noon to start writing. I was feeling so bold and confident, I even had my room door cracked a little.

After a while, a housekeeper knocked. As I had no desire for her services, I just ignored it. I think she may have even peeked in at one point, since the door wasn't fully closed, but I just kept my back to her and avoided any reaction. When she left, I got up and locked the door.

Five or ten minutes later there came another knock, more insistent. I was getting spooked but had no strategy beyond just declining to respond. Why wouldn't she just go away? Then the room phone rang. I didn't answer, and it began to dawn that my call to extend my reservation may not have been properly processed. Regardless, staff was demanding entry—a male voice hollered through the closed door at one point—and it clearly was time for me to shut down the sissy act ASAP.

I had barely enough time to throw my stuff in a pile and take a frantic shower before I got the loudest knock yet, along with voices identifying themselves as police. I don't recall whether they used a master key or waited for me to open up, but two cops were instantly in my face. Who was I? Why was I in this room that was supposed to be empty? Why had I refused entry to the hotel staff?

There was nowhere to run or hide, and no option to avoid the truth.

"This is *my* room," I said. "It's the hotel's mistake because I called this morning to extend my reservation and they said it was fine. The reason I didn't answer is because I'm a cross-dresser, and I was dressed, and I was afraid to let anybody know."

Take that, coppers.

They turned instantly from challenging to courteous. Probably they could not imagine that any man would fabricate a story about being cross-dressed, so they thanked me for my time and left. One of them even suggested that I might have a beef with the hotel. But I didn't act on that. I was still way too deep in the closet.

## CHAPTER 23

# WORLD SERIES SISSY

The year 1990 held big changes for our family. I embarked on a high-buzz new job, and we all endured the aggravation of two household moves before we landed in a brand-new home in Cincinnati's eastern suburbs. My dressing was impervious to the tumult; I found ways to get it in occasionally, and DADT still ruled for Valerie and me.

My new job was with *The Cincinnati Enquirer*. The morning paper. The number-one paper in town where I'd been looking to land since virtually day one of six-plus years at the *Post*. I had toiled for the lesser-read paper in my various cities for all sixteen years of my career, often feeling unnoticed, and now I was finally over the wall.

My last straw in working for afternoon newspapers had come in January 1990, when I scooped the *Enquirer* with the news that Bengals quarterback Boomer Esiason was declining his invite to the Pro Bowl, the NFL's postseason all-star game. I had been calling him every few days, and he confirmed it in a call on a Monday morning. We had the story in the *Post* that afternoon. The TV stations would take note and report it that evening, and the *Enquirer* would finish last for its readers with a story on Tuesday morning. But when Esiason's news came up during casual conversation in the equipment room on Tuesday, I felt sick to hear a team staffer say, "Oh yeah, I saw that in the *Enquirer* this morning."

Our two household moves developed from a reluctant decision to leave The Cove. Our brood of five had outgrown the house. But the timing of our sale forced us into a two-month rental while our new place in the suburban Eastgate area of Greater Cincinnati was completed, and as if it weren't crazy enough to be rootless during my job transition, the new gig came with a huge last-minute surprise. Just days before my July 10 start date, I was asked to take over as the *Enquirer's* baseball writer.

I had previously agreed to only a vague job description, so happy was I just to be there, and the offer stunned me. The *Enquirer* Reds beat was a prime Cincinnati media job, and though I knew I had proven my beat reporting ability with my work for the *Post,* I wasn't expecting such a vote of confidence so quickly. It was immensely gratifying. But baseball beats were known in the industry as home-wreckers, since the writer would spend a month at spring training in Florida or Arizona before following the team on multicity road trips from April into October. At thirty-eight, with three kids, I had come to assume I would never cover baseball as a beat guy.

The Reds, however, were hotter than the midsummer weather, suddenly the favorites to win the National League, and my new boss, sports editor Greg Noble, told me he wasn't comfortable with his incumbent Reds writer. He asked if I'd commit to covering the team for the rest of 1990 and all of '91. Then we could talk about something with less time on the road, possibly a return to the Bengals beat. This was a landmark in my career, and Valerie agreed that I couldn't afford to decline.

The Reds went on to win not only the National League, but the World Series—in a four-game sweep of the heavily favored Oakland Athletics. As lead writer for the biggest of the three papers that truly did cover the team every day, I became an occasional interview subject myself. My profile kept rising after the Series trophy was secured, as the *Enquirer* capitalized on Reds mania by putting mock-ups of my byline stories on all manner of clothing, coffee mugs, and posters. With the increased attention came a greater certainty that my hypothetical outing would create even bigger problems and gossip.

My baseball job did not wreck our home—the five of us handled it just fine—and as soon as I had settled in, my girl stuff was with me on the road again.

The Reds' schedule from July onward was top-heavy with California trips, and there was a Los Angeles shop catering to CDs that I wanted to visit. I wasn't sure what to expect when I made it there, but it turned out to be completely low-key outside and inside. Set in a strip mall among dentists, insurance agents, and other small retail shops, it was likely unnoticed by much of its own neighborhood. It was just like a small women's store, with a couple of clerks (both apparently cisgender women) who took my entrance as completely unremarkable.

I wasn't going to spend a fortune. Though my CD guilt level was always relatively low, spending a lot on girl stuff exacerbated it. But I had my eye on one thing in particular: my first-ever pair of breast forms.

The forms were foam rubber, extremely primitive compared to the luscious silicone forms I have today, but they had little fake nipples and were a big step up. When I modeled them in my hotel room, I was delighted to see that they imparted a more realistic shape. And when worn with a thin-fabric bra and top, the nipples protruded just a bit. It was another new and wonderful way to feel like a girl.

In our new home, I dressed when I could, but it was getting harder. Sarah, who was ten when we moved in, was getting old enough to make privacy harder to secure. Also, it was harder to get out of the house than it had been in The Cove. We were at the end of a cul-de-sac again, but it was a longer drive out, and we knew people in various homes all along the way, including the kids' friends.

My time as *Enquirer* Reds writer did not extend beyond the spring of 1991, at which point my switching back to the Bengals beat was approved. But the Bengals beat turned out to be short lived as well. After three seasons, in January of 1994, I would cross over and start working for the team.

## CHAPTER 24

# ON THE TEAM

My official hire to become the Bengals' public relations director came barely seventy-two hours after I had given the team's owner, Mike Brown, a D-minus grade in the *Enquirer*'s end-of-season analysis of a last-place campaign.

Fortunately for me, Mike took criticism less personally than most sports execs. He said he considered me a polished writer and he felt I'd been fair when my reporting was critical.

Within a couple weeks I was working in an office at Riverfront Stadium, the Bengals home that predated their 2000 move into Paul Brown Stadium. My former desks at the *Enquirer* and *Post* were just blocks away. For the next twenty-four years, I would be a cross-dressing queer embedded with a pro football team, granted 24/7 access to player areas, coaches' floors, and management suites. I worked 467 of the 468 Bengals games (including preseason) during my tenure, my one missed contest occurring when we were called to Texas by the death of Valerie's dad in September of 2016.

I was boss of our press box for every home game and boss of the visiting team section at road games. I was with the team in the locker room before and immediately after games. My capable aides, assistant director PJ Combs and PR assistant Ingrid "Inky" Moore, joined me in handling endless media issues and in forming the franchise's front line for calls from the general public. We produced reams of football information for media and were tasked with getting players to fulfill NFL-mandated media responsibilities. As had been the case in my reporting days, I had daily interaction with prominent players. A partial list drawn from both of my career phases would include Cris Collinsworth, Boomer Esiason, Anthony Muñoz, Terrell Owens, James Harrison, Chad "Ochocinco" Johnson, Adam "Pacman" Jones, Ken Anderson, Carson Palmer, Corey Dillon, and Elbert "Ickey" Woods. My two-phase span covered the tenures of six Bengals head coaches—Forrest Gregg, Sam Wyche, Dave Shula, Bruce Coslet, Dick LeBeau, and Marvin Lewis. Also, during my reporting days, I formed a relationship with Mike Brown's father, Paul, a hall-of-fame coach with the Cleveland Browns who later founded and also coached the Bengals.

From late July through early January, PJ and I joined the rest of the "football side"—top management, coaches, athletic trainers, and equipment managers—in working seven-day weeks. We'd get maybe five true days off in five months. When the team didn't do well and Mike Brown was barraged with critical letters from fans, I'd help him draft diplomatic replies. Of all the tasks I performed that directly affected him, I think he appreciated this one above all.

Hiding my CD side as a Bengal was not so different than hiding it as a journalist. The only real difference was that I was forced to quit dressing on road trips. We flew jam-packed charters to road games, so no one was allowed to check a bag. There was no time to dress anyway. The bigger CD issue as the '90s rolled into the 2000s was the advancing ages of our kids and the damper that was putting on my desires.

In this new macho environment of an NFL team, Val began to worry more and more that I would get fired if the truth about my dressing ever got out.

"Let go just for dressing?" I'd say. "No way."

But I had to admit that the optics of me—the guy who'd spent years working in the Bengals locker room—exposed as a sissy after coming in contact with hundreds of players, maybe even a thousand or more, were scary to think about.

How would a football fraternity like that handle the reveal that I was queer?

For sure there would be no kindred souls for me among the playing or coaching brotherhood. There were no openly LGBTQ+ players in any of the four major men's US pro sports during the bulk of my Bengals career, and by the end there had been only one—Jason Collins, a longtime National Basketball Association reserve who bravely outed himself in 2013, at the tail end of a thirteen-season career. The NFL made headlines in 2014 when the St. Louis Rams drafted an openly gay linebacker, Michael Sam of Missouri, but Sam never made the regular season playing roster in tries with the Rams and later the Cowboys. I thought Sam was given a fair football chance, but gay friends have insisted otherwise, that a player of Sam's ability with no known queer baggage would have made it for a while with some team. Regardless, neither he nor any other queer had cracked the NFL's straight ceiling.

As for openly queer coaches in the major sports, there were none.

"But you've gotta realize," I'd continue to Val, "even if somebody with the Bengals did find out about me, it's not like they'd be inclined to do anything about it. They might tell somebody else, and maybe it gets around, but no one would push this to a confrontation. Remember what I've told you about those players we had who were widely rumored to be gay?"

Plenty of us around the Bengals—staff as well as media—had heard rumors about gay players over the years. I never knew anything firsthand, but once it hit the grapevine you couldn't ignore it.

I clearly recall three Bengals who made this rumor circuit, and I knew from personal conversations with top management that in at least two cases, my bosses were keenly aware of the scuttlebutt. Once, before a session with media, I tried to prepare one of these players for possible questions about his sexuality, because talk about it was rampant at that time on social media.

It was a delicate assignment.

"Ahhh...I know there's...ahhh...some stuff out there about you," I stammered to the player. "And I just, uh...I wanted to remind you...you don't have to answer any questions that aren't about football. And we can support you on that."

He wordlessly conveyed that he had no idea what I was talking about, and no one ended up questioning him about it.

For other players and the coaches, the MO for dealing with these rumors was always DADT.

"But you're not a player," Val would say. "You're more expendable."

Then I'd remind Valerie that Mike Brown was not a rabid social conservative. Though up in years and a wealthy Republican, he was largely live-and-let-live in personal matters. Mike never stood in the way of my penchant for writing pointedly liberal letters and op-eds, often supporting LGBTQ+ issues, to the *Enquirer*. Mike read the *Enquirer* daily and would usually note it to me when he saw one of my efforts, and though he rarely agreed, he didn't seem to worry that conservative fans might recognize my name and complain that a Bengals spokesman should keep his public utterances focused on football.

Still, my job required me to be in the locker room a lot. Though not noticeably homophobic during the course of an average day, the Bengals' "team space" was still heavily defined by an unspoken code of tough-guy straightness, and homo-freakouts did occur occasionally.

The most durable form of harassment, seemingly carried down through player generations, involved accusing a male media member or team staffer of being a "pecker checker." Or, less poetically, a "meat gazer." A player, claiming visual violation to all within earshot, would express anything from amusement to outrage. As media manager, it would be part of my job to attempt to maintain decorum, and I would often go to the accusing player, asking what the heck specifically he was talking about. In every case the player failed to impart any credible charges.

As much as I tried to calm Valerie's anxiety on the matter, I couldn't deny that, should the players get wind that their PR director liked wearing dresses and oh-just-the-prettiest makeup, my job situation might indeed become untenable.

## CHAPTER 25

# A PROPER NEIGHBORHOOD

Even as no one from the Bengals or my world of media friends could know about my cross-dressing, people outside those worlds were slowly starting to learn about me.

My CD side was advancing every minute—even if I didn't quite sense it—toward safer spaces and more freedom. Around 1998, glacial progress started turning to gradual, and there was even an occasional gallop. The key factors were my "sheer stubbornness," as Valerie would describe it, and my successful campaign to move us back to the city from the suburbs.

I'm not a suburbs person. They're conservative by nature, and you can't vote on city issues, and it was harder to enjoy the city's entertainment options at the end of a workday when I was already downtown but the family was twenty miles away.

In '98, after eighteen or so months of my pushing the idea, Valerie agreed to pursue a move. Valerie was amenable even when I pushed the envelope by suggesting we not return to the general neighborhood of The Cove, which is in the city but lies outside the true urban core. I was intrigued by the city's Clifton neighborhood by the University of Cincinnati, less than five miles from downtown.

Clifton offered a great mix of well-to-do charm and urban grit. We eventually agreed upon a very interesting and very old house (built in

1885) that was two to three blocks from a business strip with a grocery, restaurants, bars, coffee houses, and clothing stores. The scale of it all was intimate, as the avenue had just one lane each way, and just as close to us sat a huge city park.

It was all just too perfect, except that no other kids lived on our street. Valerie was not so long in second-guessing about that, telling me I had pushed too soon for the move. She lamented that Tim and Hannah, ages eleven and nine, should have had one more year in their familiar neighborhood and pleasant school. She said I had been "selfish." (Sarah had been sixteen when we moved and was all for it.)

"Time will tell about Tim and Hannah," I'd reply to Valerie. And in the meantime, I was going to reap full enjoyment from urban life's daily tonic. And as I got to know Clifton better, it began to dawn that I lived in possibly the best neighborhood in town for a CD. It was eminently walkable and had a longtime reputation as liberal and funky. A guy who lived there had told me with a chuckle, "It's the best place to live in the whole city, as long as you can stand all the homos."

"Homos" of course presented no problem for me, and Clifton's walkability soon had me doing something new—clip-clopping in heels and skirts around my own neighborhood. At first I'd do it only late at night, and only on mostly darkened residential blocks. I wasn't brave enough to visit the business strip, which stayed lively until about midnight.

The factors of neighbors and kids also restricted me. I didn't want neighbors seeing me leave or enter the house en femme, and at that time the kids were not yet clued in. Sarah lived only a couple years in Clifton, moving out after finishing high school, but Tim and Hannah weren't going anywhere. I had to wait until they were in bed even for a late-night quickie walk, and when I wanted to dress and go out more fully, I had to pack up my stuff and drive to the home of a gay male couple I knew from church. They were always happy to let me use their place as a base of operations for an evening.

I grew braver with time. I began venturing down the business strip, sometimes alone and sometimes walking our dog. The realization had grown that Clifton people were not going to do a suburban-style bug-eye at the sight of a cross-dresser. They were used to seeing all manner of queer types, as well as panhandlers and other street people, and this mix was not only tolerated, it was quietly celebrated.

I'm not saying I never got harassed. A time or two, or three, phobics in cars passing through the strip would yell, "Die, you fag!" or stuff like that. But there was almost no trouble with anyone on foot. Though Clifton businesses and attractions drew visitors from less progressive areas, they would generally keep their place because they weren't on their safe turf.

And darned if I didn't come to learn that one of the bars on Ludlow was a gay establishment. I swear I knew nothing of it when we chose the house, but I came to learn that the Golden Lions Lounge was touted by some as the oldest gay bar in the city. It certainly was old-school in its exterior signage, as there was none. It harked to the days when those who ought to know about a gay bar already did, and others were best left unapprised.

I didn't initially consider going inside, but I liked going by the door on my dressed walks. I figured that anyone walking in or out would be passably friendly, and I was of course curious about the place even when in male clothes.

Before too long, though, I was to become a regular at the Lions. The turning point came when I saw what appeared to be another cross-dresser outside the place, standing among a few folks taking a smoke break.

# THE CD LIFE: THE TUCK

Nothing is everything.

That's my motto for the all-important "flat front" look in presenting as a woman, and I don't mean a flat belly. I want that, too—that's what corsets are for—but in this case we're talking about a flat front in the crotch area, with no hint of a male bulge.

What could be more feminine, after all, than not having a penis?

"The Tuck" requires the shoving of one's male parts back between one's thighs and then securing the flesh so it can't find a way to emerge even when you're moving about. It's not so hard to do with the proper simple equipment: a well-fitting pair of bikini panties and some very tight elastic shorts. "Gaffs" are panties ostensibly designed for this purpose, but I've never found them effective. They're not unlike a thong, and in my experience, they just don't have enough fabric to properly contain the equipment.

Regular bikini panties perform much better for me, but they can't do it alone. The key is the very small elastic shorts, which I've learned to find in the young girls' section of Target or Meijer stores. I guess young girls wear these as actual shorts, but for me they're an undergarment, and I try to get the smallest possible size that I can pull up over my butt and thighs. Rule of thumb: If it's not a titanic struggle to get 'em on, especially the first time, they're not small enough to provide optimal protection against something slipping out. While holding in your tucked equipment, you pull your panties up as high as they'll reasonably go and then pull the shorts much less reasonably, yanking with savage intensity to smooth the fabric over the space where your maleness used to be.

Voilà! You have created the impression there must be a vulva under there. What a turn-on, and it's not at all uncomfortable once you get used to it. It's almost as if nature designed a space for times when your equipment is not to be seen or acknowledged. Pantyhose can also aid in this effort, but the panties and shorts should be enough if you're wanting to go bare-legged.

I once had a pair of lacy white shorts that drew consistent compliments from women, even though there was nothing particularly flashy about them, and I eventually came to discern what must have been the attraction: the shorts formed just the cutest little flat triangle, exactly where you'd want it to be.

## CHAPTER 26

# LURED TO THE LIONS

Two or three sightings of the cross-dresser outside the Golden Lions were needed for me to exhaust all my little reasons for procrastinating. When I finally resolved to engage, I was in male clothes, walking our dog. I said hi and told her I was also of the transgender community. She was unhesitatingly friendly and encouraged me to get dolled up myself and drop in soon.

So I did. I was terribly excited in anticipation of my first visit to the Lions. Nothing went awry, so for a long period I'd go maybe once a week. Valerie found some comfort in knowing I'd be only three blocks away and not driving after drinking.

I got to know Marie (not her real name), the smoker who'd encouraged me to visit, and also a crowd who hung around with her. I figured they must be all kind of queer in some way, but Marie was the only outwardly transgendered one. I learned that although I'd assumed she was a CD much like myself, she was actually much more a true transsexual, living nearly 24/7 as a woman and pondering transition surgery.

On the whole, I still wasn't very friendly with the crowd. Mostly I'd just sit at the bar and interact a little with others near me. This relative lack of sociability, and the resultantly shallow relationships, were of my own doing. Despite my strong urge to be dressed in public, I rather liked the fantasy feeling of being a lone sissy in a bar full of curious strangers, and I was still seriously scared about unwittingly revealing my true identity.

When people asked about my life outside the bar, I'd give it up that I was married with kids and that I worked "in public relations." No real name, no home address, and certainly nothing about working for the Bengals or even my sportswriting. But even in a queer alcove like this, football could rear its head.

"Are you a Bengals fan?" Marie asked me one September night a few years after I first started coming to the bar. She'd been discussing the team's most recent game with another regular, a guy who usually was there as "Mike" but had once or twice come as "Michelle." Mike/Michelle and Marie often talked about the Bengals.

"Usually they are frustrating as hell," Marie went on about my employers, "but I really think they're gonna be good this year. Do you follow 'em at all?"

"Oh yeah," I said. "I keep track of 'em."

"I went to their game at Cleveland last year," said Mike.

*I was at that game, too,* I wanted to say. *I've gone to every game home and away for like 15 years.*

"Sounds like a fun trip" was what I actually said.

"I like going to training camp," Mike said. "You can really get up close to the players. I got Palmer's autograph this year. I took off work. He was really nice."

*I was at camp for three weeks and didn't have to miss work,* I didn't say. *I'm the one who reminded Carson Palmer after practice that he needed to go sign for you fans.*

Nope. Couldn't say any of that.

Reds baseball would come up, too. I took pains not to note that I'd been on the Reds beat for the 1990 World Series.

I regretted that I couldn't open up with these folks. I was proud of my career in sports and loved it that most friends liked to hear me hold forth as an insider. But Jack the sports guy simply could not also be Jack who adores cute heels. A definite split-personality deal, that.

Sometimes bar patrons I didn't know would be curious about me and invite me to join their table. When people asked for more specifics about my "public relations" job, I first tried falsely using the name of a big downtown PR firm. That proved not an effective lie, as the firm had too many connections in the community.

"I just heard about them doing that big remodel," a lady noted. "How do you like the new space?"

"Very nice," I said. And thank God right then that my wineglass was nearly empty. "I'm headed to the bar! Who needs a drink?"

I took it as a fluke, until it happened again.

"Oh, my friend works there!" said a girl. "What's your name? I'll tell her we met. What department do you work in?"

This time my wineglass was full, but you'll never see a CD more suddenly develop an overpowering need to go pee.

From that point on, I met job questions with just my truth.

"You know," I'd say, "given my situation, I'm just not comfortable offering any more on it."

Good move. People seemed to accept that. No one ever gave me the feeling they were bent on ratting me out.

It was, however, all quite unsatisfying interpersonally. Also, I didn't like leading people to assume I was a corporate business PR type. In the sports PR community, as well as in sports journalism, we always saw ourselves as far cooler than buttoned-up business types.

Other questions I'd field centered on how cross-dressing could mix with a "straight" marriage. Did this threaten the marriage? Was Valerie really supportive? Did she ever come up to the bar?

At least I could be honest about those queries. I'd tell people that Valerie found it in herself to tolerate my feminine side, that she was more supportive than not, and that we had talked about her visiting the bar with me, though that visit never ended up happening.

So the Lions became a home base for me, despite my less than robust friendships there, and as my comfort level increased, I warmed to a new challenge: karaoke.

It was my first karaoke anywhere. I would strut before an audience in heels and sexy clothes and makeup, performing a tune that only a girl would sing. I'd sing sweetly, I prayed.

Finding the right song for karaoke was a challenge, as I wasn't conversant with the recent stuff that dominated the DJ's offerings, but I wound up happy with a selection of "It's in His Kiss," first released back in the '60s but re-popularized by Cher in the early '90s. That's the version I remembered, and I practiced it in my basement over the course of several days, able to play it on my smart phone.

In my early rehearsals, I tried to make my male voice sound more feminine, but it just didn't work. I sounded like what I was—a man profoundly failing in an attempt to sing like a girl. I knew that men could attain a female pitch on demand with proper training, as I had once borrowed an instructional recording for it from a CD support group. But the recording made it clear that many hours of work would be required for a desirable result, and I never had been up for the effort.

Soon it was the night of my performance. Upon turning in my request, I felt that "Aha!" moment when one has stepped past a point of no return. It felt scary, forbidden, and foolish, but I also felt sheer excitement. With my slot still some minutes away, I went outside to slam down a cigarette.

Finally, my call came. I probably didn't sing too well or too sexily that first time out, but the crowd was supportive. I felt affirmed, and I knew I would do it again. I often asked fellow patrons (only the women) to video my performance on my phone. I came to regard getting the video as essential, and thus I would fret until I could find a shooter. But somehow, I always did.

## CHAPTER 27

# OUT TO THE KIDS

When I joined the Bengals, Sarah was thirteen, Tim seven, and Hannah five. It was hard enough to get pretty while negotiating Val's up-and-down acceptance level, and now there were three live-in humans fully afoot who couldn't be allowed to know.

What would I say if a child happened onto my stuff? Worse yet, what if a "secure" time to indulge proved otherwise and a kid stumbled upon CD Dad in flagrante delicto? Confusion and fear would surely result.

I was in denial for years, however, about the need to take action. I was too scared and sick over the big gulp of telling my kids I was a queer. Instead, I was accepting small sips of fear every day and whistling down a dangerous road.

Valerie to the rescue. She never came to me about the need to do something, she just took upon herself a service that might seem too implausibly perfect were this a work of fiction. When I was not around, she opened up for me, and about me, to each kid at what seemed the right moment.

I had no advance knowledge of her disclosures because none were planned. Valerie's life wisdom comes mostly from gut instinct, and if I asked her today whether she perceived I was emotionally unable to take action on an important issue, I know she'd say she doesn't even remember.

Her process started in late 2003, with our youngest, Hannah, who was then fourteen.

"Mom told me about you when I was writing a paper for school," Hannah has told me. "My topic was why gay marriage should be made legal. I was on the computer you guys used to have in your bedroom, and Mom was on the bed, about to take a nap.

"We were talking about my paper, and then Mom asked, 'What would you do if you discovered one of your parents was transgendered?' I'm not sure how we got to that particular question, but I said it wouldn't matter and I would love them the same. Then she told me you liked cross-dressing and would do it occasionally. I was pretty shocked. But in hindsight I had seen things like a wig catalog in the mail. I knew Mom had no interest in wigs, and it always puzzled me that we got those."

It was 2018 when Hannah recounted that story to me. I was asking all three kids and Valerie for their memories of the process.

Although Hannah had been the first to be clued in by Valerie, Sarah told me that she had figured it out long before that, in 1990. She said she just never told us or questioned us about it.

"I was about ten when I first knew," Sarah said.

> We had just moved into the brand-new house, and the move was a big adventure for me. I remember being in the basement, and there was a box of women's clothes. I thought it was odd, since they weren't the types of clothes Mom would wear. Well, I was never one to let a mystery sit idle, and I dug further until I found a wig and a box of letters. And I read a letter you had written to Diane. I remember being very sad, as it alluded to struggles you faced. Then I put everything back.
>
> During the next couple days, I tried to sort it all out. I didn't understand much about what you did or why, but I did understand that this wasn't something new. It was a part of who you were, so in a way it didn't change anything. I knew a secret without you knowing—you know I love that kind of thing—and for me it became like one of the old books on our shelf. It had always been there, and it would always be there, gathering dust and ready to be opened when it was your time to share it with me.

That was all news to me. When Val tried to tell her, just a week or two after she had told Hannah, Sarah said she already knew.

"She said, 'I promise, you don't know this,' but then I told her, and she was very shocked," Sarah said.

The precise circumstances of Tim's "Moment with Mom" have escaped all our memories, but he was likely about sixteen.

"I just kind of remember Mom mentioning it to me one day and being like, 'Oh, OK, that's sort of weird, but I still love him,'" says Tim.

Valerie says, "All I really remember is that I told each one when I thought the time was right." Though the hardest part had been done for me, I still needed to talk individually with each kid.

"So, Sarah," I said to my eldest. "I know Mom tried to tell you about me being a cross-dresser, and I know you said you already knew for a long time. But still, I just want to make sure you feel OK about everything."

Sarah no longer lived with us and was to be married within weeks. It wasn't like I was trying to explain this to a little kid. But the reckoning still made me queasy.

"It's fine," she said. "I really don't have a problem with it. You have to be you."

Hannah and Tim were still in-home adolescents.

"It's OK, Dad," Hannah said. "You're a good dad and that's all that matters. You've raised us to be inclusive of people."

"Do you, uh, have any questions I could try to answer?"

"No, not really."

And then I let her be, breathing a sigh.

Tim also had no further questions. It had been all I could to do to get his attention away from a video game.

I guess you're not all that eager to give your dad the third degree when you learn he does something most folks consider weird. What you really want is just some loving support, some reassurance that the parent remains fundamentally unchanged from the one you have always known.

With their acceptance, my personal evolution continued.

CHAPTER 28

# THE BEAUTIFUL BE-ALL

Valerie's coming out to the kids on my behalf was not only immensely loving and helpful, it signaled that some thirty years after learning about me, she had reached a significant acceptance level of her mate. My read is that, like the kids, she had just needed reassurance there weren't deep cracks in our foundation. It had come oh-so-gradually, but I came to know that, should a genie offer to change me with just a wink, she would decline.

"That part of you vanishing would make you not the same person I fell in love with," she once told me, "even though I didn't know about that part at the time."

Val's devotion to the whole me was never displayed more emphatically than when she accompanied me to Chicago for the 2004 Be-All, a weekend convention for the transgender diaspora.

It shocks me still that she was willing to go. I had offhandedly floated the idea some six weeks previously, with no more hope of winning than a Mega Millions buyer. I figured it was worth it just to educate her that such things existed. Maybe it would lay some groundwork for a possible future visit.

But damned if she didn't say yes and add, "I know it means a lot to you to be able to go to something like this, and I want to support you. And you know me, I'm always up for a mini vacation."

It truly was a heartwarming moment for us as a couple. Too bad we had to hide it from 98 percent of our world. But that was life as a CD. You can sometimes briefly forget what you're hiding 24/7, but it's never long before it smacks you upside the head.

"What are you going to do if Tami calls you this weekend?"

It was the day before our departure for Chicago, and I was asking Val about her younger sister. Tami and her family presented a particularly knotty problem for this trip, because they lived in the northern Chicago suburbs, and it seemed very weird, perhaps even dishonest, to be so near their home and not try at all to see them.

Tami actually knew about me already. Val had told her years ago. But the disclosure had been brief, and they'd never discussed it since. Matt, Tami's husband, came from a conservative Filipino family. Though we loved Matt dearly and knew him as more liberal than much of his family, he always seemed a bit to the right of Tami. And—crucially— we doubted Tami had clued him in on her knowledge of me.

Val and I went back and forth about plans and cover-ups, none of which were satisfying. After all that, we wound up with no plan, just rolling the dice on Tami not calling. And she didn't, but the stress of worrying about it had already registered.

The Be-All drew roughly 150 attendees to a hotel in Chicago's western suburbs. It included merchandise displays, informational sessions, side trips to the Boystown gay district, and a banquet. The crowd was welcoming, not a bit off-putting to Valerie. We attendees all had some form of shared experience, and it showed in the overall warmth.

I dressed in our room, and Valerie not only accepted that, she *helped*. It was just with a few minor wardrobe issues, but bless her dear heart that I love so much, she wanted me to look nice—and to feel good about looking nice. Though this was not at all the first time she'd seen me fully dressed, it was the first time she had seen me dressed in earnest, not under the guise of a bit or a performance like the Halloween party. And it was the first instance of any *teamwork*, of dressing being something that at least for a special occasion was a shared endeavor. I was not subject to the disapproval, even if unspoken, that had overlaid many previous opportunities, even when she had officially said it was OK.

Meeting the other attendees was interesting for both of us. We were charmed and touched by a couple with a transgender daughter about age eight. Assigned male at birth, she now lived as a girl, fully supported by her parents. This was clearly a happy child, not one emotionally crushed by rejection and guilt. Her parents spoke at one of the presentations, and the child became the unofficial mascot of the event.

We also had a sobering lunchtime conversation with a couple whose situation bore similarities to our own. They seemed about our age, had been married many years, and appeared comfortably middle class. The wife had long known her husband was a CD, and though it wasn't her cup of tea, she had chosen to stay with the person she loved and not let the dressing define their relationship. Sound familiar?

But over dessert, it came out that their one child, an adult daughter, was under instruction to never visit their home without calling in advance. Unlike our kids, she didn't know about her dad. The couple conceded that the directive was awkward, an ongoing source of puzzled concern to the daughter. But they were steadfast regarding their intention to offer her no further explanation.

Most marvelously at the Be-All, Valerie encouraged my purchasing my first set of silicone breast forms, a game-changing advance in dressing. I already had a foam rubber pair, but silicone was so much more realistic.

"Did you see the vendor's booth?" she asked.

For sure I had, but I hadn't seen them as being for me. How could I justify spending big bucks on a pair of fake tits?

"You ought to just go check them out. You don't know how much they are until you ask."

She actually was saying that. I wasn't hallucinating. And she said she'd go with me.

Val took the lead with the vendor, a nice cisgender woman. Everybody was nice at this event. No one seemed to be out to scam anybody.

"See what you think of these," Val was saying. I had come down wearing a bra, but flat-chested, no socks inside.

The feeling was distinctive, shall we say. The silicone forms were a little cold, but very soft. And heavy.

The vendor brought out a bigger pair, which I immediately liked better.

"Are you sure?" Val said. "Will they fit under all your clothes? Some women wouldn't mind if their boobs were a little smaller."

"They fit OK under this blouse," I said, "and I'm not small in the shoulders and the chest. I think they're in proportion."

So the bigger size it was. There was never any question I was getting a pair, and Val processed the payment. I never knew how much they cost. Valerie still didn't want to bring my dressing intimately into our lives, but she knew I needed to dress.

What she didn't know—nor did I, truly—was what I'd do when I flew solo at the 2005 Be-All.

# THE CD LIFE: BRALESS

Nothing can more quickly ruin a CD evening than having one of your tits fall off.

It has happened to me a few times, but hopefully never will again. Although I still love to go braless with my soft silicone breast forms, I've gotten better over time at making them securely a part of me.

The essential starting step is shaving my chest to absolute max smoothness. The instructions for the adhesive basically scold, "Don't even THINK of trying this over stubble." I have to shave from several different angles to catch the grain of the hair just right, and I've got to be careful shaving around those nipples.

My adhesive of choice is double-sided tapes, made for this purpose by a wonderful online place called The Breast Form Store. Prior to the attachment, I also use alcohol-based towelettes to make the flesh tacky.

The tapes should be applied over only the top three or four inches of the inside of the breast form. Beginners might be tempted to affix the form entirely, but the breasts must be allowed to flop freely at the bottom, so as to adjust to normal body movement. Once the breasts go on, I wear a bra for at least thirty minutes to firm up the bond, and then the bra comes off. It's always an exciting moment to see and feel your breasts holding their own, just as if they were a real girl's! Only very rarely in my later dressing years have I worn a bra out of the house. It feels just so feminine to have my soft breasts wiggling a little under a soft and flimsy top when I walk.

But there's always a level of anxiety, because once a form falls off, you can't restick it without major work at home. You can always carry an emergency bra, and I have on occasion, but that's kind of a drag. Summer is the most dangerous season for braless presentation, as heat and humidity can weaken the adhesive bond. I try to carry a battery-operated mini-fan with me when it's hot, and sometimes I'll go to the ladies' room, where I'll lift up my top and direct some air under the unattached part of the breasts, to cool and dry the taped area.

Once at the bar a guy asked me in all apparent seriousness, "Are those [breasts] really real?" I told him, of course, that they were.

CHAPTER 29

# KISSING MR. WRONG

**V**alerie and I both felt good about our Be-All experience. The very fact of her attendance was more than I had ever expected, and she called it "fun and interesting." But when I inquired the following summer about doing it again, Val was in "been there, done that" mode. She told me I could go alone if I wanted to, and I did. But I wound up acting poorly, taking advantage of her trust.

On the first day, after waking up at 3:30 a.m. to arrive in time to not miss a thing, I attended a happy-hour cocktails session. I wore a tight jean skirt and a clingy top that showed off my realistic breasts, and not only did my figure look so much better than it once had, so did my legs. Though I still felt not at liberty to shave, having done it only that one time more than twenty years previously, I had covered my hair with tan opaque tights under sheer hose.

I made conversation with other CDs, feeling fairly comfortable. But a man, the only person in male garb in the room, was also noticeably making the rounds. He was an African American about my age, not a great looker but not a slob, and though it appeared he had a steady sissy girlfriend with him, he was being quite friendly with us other CDs as well. Too friendly, really, and that was what quickly caught my eye.

I harbor the conceit that I looked pretty hot, relatively speaking. I had always thought myself better looking than most cross-dressers. I worked out regularly, I was acceptably slim, and since tan opaque hose, my legs sparked women's envy wherever I went. As a man, I had been regularly told I didn't look my age. So I like to think this guy was attracted to me over others in the room. Soon he was laying his spiel on me.

"Helloooo! So glad to see you. My name is Ronald. And yours, if I may?"

"Sissy," I said, with what I hoped was a nice smile. I still had not arrived on a permanent femme name and had just picked this one out for the Be-All because it sounded so...well, you know.

"Sissy, you're very pretty," Ronald crooned, "and I just have to say how much I love all the beauty on display in this room."

I thanked him for considering me a part of that. A bit of small talk followed. Then, "I think what I love most is all the beautiful shoes you ladies wear; I have to admit to being a little bit of a foot fetishist, I guess."

"Nothing wrong with that," I said, heart rather thudding.

"But I know those heels must be hard on your feet sometimes, and it just so happens that I give the world's greatest foot rubs. May I offer you one? I've already done it for some other ladies and I think they'd give me good reviews."

I was a big fan of foot rubs. I'd never given them high marks for eroticism, but I was willing to play along. I slipped off a heel and put one leg in Ronald's lap. He was a good massager indeed. The physical contact of it wasn't a turn-on, but it was pleasant enough.

"There's something about the feel of feet through nylon hose," he said. "It's just so feminine. And I like your shoes. Thank you for wearing those tonight."

"Oh these?" I cooed. "I like 'em, too, but they're really just a pair of daytime heels."

I was getting into this. Couldn't be denied. Ron was on the prowl, and I didn't mind.

"You know, I have a cuter pair in my room," I said. "Higher heel, more of an evening shoe. I could go up and put those on, would you like to see those?"

*Affirmative.*

I entered my room in a 100 percent brand-new mental space. I was yielding to temptation and dressing for a man. I took a hit of pot and paused to just ponder it. Then I put on those cuter heels and headed back to happy hour.

"Those are so sexy on you," Ronald decided. "Let me admire those just for a minute and then I'll rub your other foot."

My feminine wiles were appealing to this person with a penis between his legs. What fun. But I was never going to take this too far, and after a bit more foot rub, I reached my limit for his bullshit and found a way to free him to pursue other prey. I was still a bit horny for him, though, and we concurred that we would surely cross paths again during the weekend. His ties to his sissy girlfriend were obviously loose. She even told me before I left the happy hour, "He thinks you're really cute."

*What would it feel like to kiss him?*

I asked myself that on Saturday morning. By lunchtime, I knew I would offer him that chance during the group banquet that evening. Of course we managed to be tablemates, and of course he was all in.

"You've gotta know I'm not into anything really serious," I warned.

When the desserts were cleared, we repaired to a vacant table in a partially darkened part of the ballroom. We sat close and kissed. Nothing deep, he really was quite polite, but our tongues touched a couple times, and I enjoyed it. But after maybe two minutes, I determined it was time to gently disengage.

Ron was not ready to call it quits. "I have a bottle of hundred-year-old cognac in my room," he said. "What do you think of going up there and getting to know each other a little better? Or I could bring it to your room."

"No, remember, I'm not up for anything serious," I said. "You're a nice guy, but I told you, I'm married. I wouldn't do that with anybody. It's nothing personal."

He accepted without protest.

I had no illusions about Ronald. Despite his civility, he struck me as someone who felt cross-dressers were an easy and submissive route to cheap sex. I imagined that he might be quite a different person, and not in a good way, behind closed doors. But I was using him for my own purposes, just as he was trying to use me for his. I was using him to satisfy my curiosity about flirting with a man. He had to make do with less than he'd hoped for, and I suspect that surprised him.

I did wonder about the CD—or maybe she was actually transitioning—who presented as Ron's girlfriend. She was always submissively hanging back, out of the conversational stream. Her comment to me about Ron liking my looks was the only outreach I saw her make to anyone, and though she clung to Ron when he was close, he paid her little attention when others were around. When he and I had slipped away from the banquet table, he left without a word to her, as if she wasn't even there. When we returned, I tried to make eye contact with her, but her gaze was downcast. She was the only one left at our table; the others who had dined with us had already departed. Ron's interaction with her was neither apologetic nor warm.

"Let's get upstairs," he curtly told her, and then they were gone.

It was easy to envision that she had landed with this character after being ostracized by family and former friends.

I feel bad in hindsight for potentially having helped enable Ron's disdainful—or even abusive—ways. But at the time, his girl was just a character in my fantasy play. I don't even remember her name. I may not have remembered it beyond fifteen seconds, and my suspicion that she was a poor thing in a tough situation did not amount to real empathy for her. I could have tried to be her friend for forty-eight hours, tried to take an interest in who she was and how she got there. But I didn't have time for that. When I left her with Ron in that ballroom, I had work to do, planning how I would look really sexy for Ron at the Sunday morning buffet breakfast.

Ron's face lit up when he saw me. His girlfriend smiled wanly. I immediately sat next to Ron—right next to him—and sought the right feminine body language to encourage him. Already touching thighs, I made an extra ooch to intensify the contact. Above the table line, I tried to melt just a little toward him.

If Ron hadn't come to the table with the same idea, he caught on real fast. But he was gentle. Subtle.

"You can move your hand a little higher if you want," I whispered.

And he did. Just the right distance, not too far. I loved it.

Then a buzzkill. We were prompted to get up for our table's turn at the buffet. I didn't want to disengage. But in minutes we were back at it. Ron could shovel scrambled eggs just fine with only one hand, it turned out.

But his hand on my thigh was as far as it went. My private parts were all tucked back between my legs—creating a faux vagina look—and my entire groin area was encased in panties, opaque hose, and sheer hose.

All through the foot massage and the kissing and the Sunday morning gropes, I never focused on what might be going on with Ron's dick. But I liked being with a guy who wanted to fuck me. I wished we could stay and play another day.

But all too soon it was time for everyone to push back from breakfast and vacate our rooms for checkout. Ron wasn't waving the white flag just yet, though.

"Are you sure you don't want to come up for just a few minutes? We've got time, checkout isn't for an hour."

"Nope, sorry," I said. "I'm really flattered that you ask, but I'm just not going that route. It was fun to meet you, and I hope you guys have a nice trip home."

Ron left me his phone number, but I didn't keep it. I felt a little bad again for Ron's sissy, but I didn't let it darken the rest of my day. I had yet another new adventure planned. I was going to drive all five hours back to Cincinnati en femme!

I called Valerie to let her know I'd be coming through the front door dressed. She was cool enough with that. But I had a confession to make. I had managed to keep Val out of my mind through most of the weekend, not wanting thoughts of her to intrude on my fantasy. But I knew in the back of my mind that I would not try to hide what had happened from her. Though my left brain knew I could say nary a word about Ron and stand a 99.8 percent chance of her never finding out, my right brain couldn't cozy to it. It was no secret between us that dressing was sexually exciting to me and that I longed to play-act the female part in social situations. But kissing a man for more than a platonic peck was over the line, and I knew that if this CD thing was going to work in our relationship, honesty was a must.

When I came downstairs, after deconstructing, to spill the truth, she was watching *Jeopardy!* Maybe I should have created the category *Kiss Another Man at a Convention* and seen if Val could come up with "What Shitty Thing Did Jack Do in Chicago?" But I wasn't feeling creative.

"Guy, I've got to tell you something that happened in Chicago."

She noticeably stiffened, turning down the TV.

"Was somebody from the Bengals at the hotel? Did somebody find you out?"

"No, it's different than that. I let somebody kiss me a little. A man who was at the Saturday night banquet. I just got carried away by the whole deal up there."

She was out of her chair now.

"Did you let him do anything else?"

"No, I swear I didn't, and the kisses weren't deep, and it was all over in like two minutes. I never was going to do anything unfaithful, and I never did. I really am sorry, I hope you'll forgive me; it was the wrong thing to do."

"I think it was crappy, even if that's all you did."

"It *was* all I did, I promise." I squeezed her hand and said, "Love Truth." It was a phrase from our courtship and early marriage years, our relational equivalent of swearing on a Bible.

"Would it seem so bad if I had flirted with a woman?" I pleaded. "If it hadn't been related to my being dressed up? You told me you used to flirt sometimes when you'd go out in Memphis. I'm just trying to be honest like you were."

She forgave me. Better yet, she did it with no extended period of being obviously wounded. She had been comfortable with the Be-All as a scene for me to further explore my need to dress, and she accepted that my mistake had not been a fundamental breach of trust, but rather one brief case of partying excess.

I did, however, pay a price beyond the painful confession. I knew that AIDS wasn't transmissible through "normal" kissing, but guilt and fear left me unable to trust that knowledge. Despite what I knew, I began to worry that I could have contracted the disease from Ronald. He seemed to perfectly fit the profile of a carrier. Oh, what a payback that would be for my indiscretion, delivering not only a deadly condition but a disgraced connection to gay sex.

I chose not to share these fears with Valerie. But I needed something to ease my mind. I called the Centers for Disease Control, not so scared to tell the truth to an anonymous voice in Atlanta. But the response proved less than sufficiently reassuring. It was, essentially, a "You're probably fine" rather than a complete bill of health.

This led me to feel I had to also contact my primary care physician, a course of action that brought on an extra level of fear. My doc was also one of the Bengals' team physicians, contracted by the club to attend all games and work with injured players. That's how I had hooked up with him in the first place, and we saw each other frequently at the stadium.

There was no way he was going to get the real story, and I didn't want to tell him anything in person. The most I could risk was a fabricated tale over email about being with a woman at a party. And since women were considered not nearly as likely as men to be AIDS carriers, I embellished the intensity of the kissing so as to make my concern seem more valid. But his response also fell short of the complete "no worries" that I craved, and it was weeks before I could get the scare completely out of my mind.

## CHAPTER 30

# THE PROBLEM WITH CUCUMBERS

As I started going out en femme more often, the worries of being caught naturally grew. Still, I kept on dressing in my free time and reverting to Mr. Football Guy at the stadium. I mixed it all into a "normal" regimen of parenting, home maintenance, time with straight friends, and recreational sports.

It wasn't that hard. That's my immediate reaction, anyway, as I look back. Through the power of human adaptability, I was able to hide it, mentally process it, and jam it seamlessly into Jack's very busy routine. Perhaps, without my being fully aware, it was one of those inexplicable true human feats. Like in *Ripley's,* you know?

I kept it all together even in the most trying circumstances, including the 2010 Monday that began uncommonly early, just after midnight, when I developed a literal pain in the ass. It was due to the piece of English cucumber—one of those really long ones—that was stuck in my rectum.

I had inserted the massive and manly vegetable as part of a masturbation exercise that followed a Sunday evening dressing session. The procedure was not altogether uncommon for me, and I had come to fancy myself quite the expert at comparing Kroger's cuke offerings for just the right length and girth. Why not just a dildo? Well, darling, these were *longer* than the rubber dicks I had. There really was nothing quite like these cukes in my history of anal penetration. I could get a shiver just holding a new one and removing the vacuum-wrapped cello.

But on this night, my selection had shown a most awful structural flaw. Facing a stress test no more arduous than a number of its predecessors had weathered intact, it snapped like a twig at my entrance point. I was left holding a five-inch section—still perfectly good for a salad or a couple sandwiches—but maybe nine more inches were lodged completely inside.

"No problem," I declared, "I'll just shit that motherfucker right out like a big turd." I was virtually addressing the intruder, about to physically impose my will. Like good football players do.

But after straining, stressing, and whimpering for maybe forty-five minutes, alternating between sitting on the toilet and standing, I was forced to concede that it was quite massively stuck. It seemed a trip to the ER was inevitable.

But at least I sort of knew what to expect, because this would be my second such trip.

Some five years previously, at the Chicago Be-All Valerie had attended, a lackluster group outing to Boystown had left me still craving excitement and ready for a deluxe jacking off.

Masturbating in girl mode didn't always include anal penetration. Sometimes it seemed just messy and not worth the hassle—but this was a special trip, and I wanted a special kick. So my dildo was on the docket, and putting all eight inches where the sun never shined was the best available outlandishly feminine thing I could do. It was a gesture of complete submission to the male sexual power—and thus it delivered the fuel for an excellent orgasm.

Once down from that, however, I discovered for the first time that what goes in sometimes prefers not to come out. I was beyond mortified at having to tell Val where I was going, and why, but she handled it amazingly well, with no shaming, only with concern about me having possibly injured myself. And I had learned an important lesson: always leave enough sticking out for a handhold.

But I hadn't ignored the lesson on the follow-up incident with the cuke, dammit. I had those five inches of it in my hand as proof. It was just that the possibility of breakage had never crossed my mind.

So, now, the ER was beckoning me again.

But wait! Maybe not. This thing wasn't made of silicone or rubber, after all. Wasn't it probably 95 percent water, with a little cellulose or some such stuff holding it together? If I could stand the discomfort for just a while, wouldn't it decompose in its 98.6-degree humid environment and just get all mushy, easy to part with forever?

It sounded like a plan. I eased myself into bed next to dear and deeply sleeping Valerie and tried to relax. I actually half-dozed for a little while. But at about 1:30 a.m. I returned to full consciousness, with the cuke not feeling any softer and hurting me more and more.

Well, fuck it, at least we lived less than half a mile from Cincinnati's Good Samaritan Hospital. I had to go there without delay.

"Wake up," I said while rustling Valerie's shoulder. "You gotta wake up just briefly..."

"UNNNHHH!!!"

I had known this would take a minute.

Her eyes were still bleary but focusing. As she gradually booted up, I realized that one aspect of this catastrophe was oddly fortunate: this wasn't Valerie's first impaled-butt-CD rodeo! What a life partner she had been that weekend, and on this night five years later, I hoped she would be the same. She didn't know of my cucumber habit, and I hated to remind her how I liked to pretend at getting fucked like a woman, but it wasn't like any of this was a revelation to her by this time.

"So it's like last time, I don't need to go with you?" she said.

"No. Just keep your phone on."

She was asleep five minutes later.

It took me all of ninety seconds to drive to Good Samaritan, and at least I knew the basic drill. I was embarrassed of course, but I was cautiously confident I'd be treated in a businesslike manner. The ER in Chicago had been that way, and all these ER people would have seen guys with worse stuff up their asses than cucumbers, right? Even sometimes hamsters, I had read.

When the admissions person said, "What can we do for you this morning?" it was no time for euphemisms.

"I've got a big piece of a cucumber stuck up my butt and I need you guys to get it out for me," I said. "Sorry to have to bother you with something like this."

"That's what we're here for," she replied, deadpan as could be. "Let me get your information, and then are you able to sit in the waiting room? We are not super crowded, but I don't have anyone available to see you just this moment."

"I think I'll be all right," I said. "I'm in some pain, but it's manageable."

"Just let us know if that changes," she said.

After about forty minutes of shifting my butt on hard plastic in search of reduced pressure, I was summoned. It was just after 2:30 a.m. I underwent an MRI to produce a visual of the situation, then I was worked over by two ER people, one guy and one girl. I don't know if they were doctors or nurses or some of those new near-doctor types. They were so matter-of-fact, I could almost imagine they were mechanics and I was a '57 Chevy with a fuel line problem.

"I can't get a grip on it with this forceps," said the girl. "Can you hand me the D-82?"

"I don't think the alignment's good," said the guy. "Sir, let's try having you lay on your other side. This thing has gone kind of sideways on us and I think it'll line up better this way."

I flopped over and braced for the next attempt.

"This thing is being just a little difficult," the girl said as I tried to stifle groans. "But hang in there, we're gonna get it."

How encouraging it was to hear that. With some assurance that they were closing in, I could much better stand the pain.

"I've got it," she finally said. The clock read 3:30 a.m.

"Just relax now; don't squeeze up on me."

Talk about blessed relief. I felt so good when it was out, I engaged in a little conversation.

"You know, I thought at first that I might not have to come up here. I thought it might just dissolve in an hour or so."

"Oh, no," said the guy. "It's not the same as it being in your stomach. There's no digestive enzymes in there to break it down. That would have taken a long time."

"Be careful now," said the girl. "Hopefully we can avoid seeing you again."

I felt kind of guilty about running up an ER bill of probably four figures and taking on only a seventy-five-dollar co-pay. The Bengals provided excellent health coverage—we didn't pay a dime in monthly fees—and some of our co-pays would even be refunded if we applied. But I wasn't going to try this one for a refund. I worried enough about our Bengals bean-counters simply reviewing account activity and seeing a description of the charge. But that hadn't happened with the Chicago visit, or at least no one had ever mentioned it, so I guessed it would be the same now.

There was no sense fretting over it, and some seven hours later, just before Monday lunchtime, I was back at the stadium, straight as could be in my Bengals polo and khakis. I had called my assistants to let them know I'd be a couple hours late, pleading an upset stomach. This was in May, the offseason, and I soberly acknowledged to myself what a major mess this could have been during the season, when Monday mornings were a crucial time for preparing our major dump of media information about the next game.

"But don't be too hard on yourself," I self-comforted. "You never would try a stunt like that during the season."

But part of me did feel terrible. It wasn't easy accepting that those gorgeous cukes could never be trusted again.

## CHAPTER 31

# HOME SWEET ARLIN'S

The Golden Lions remained a good enough haven for me for seven or eight years, but in late 2010, patrons learned that the place was in trouble. Poor management had led to a nightmarish tangle of debt, the bartenders said, and in June of '11, the day came when the doors just didn't open. A scrawled sign said the closure would be only temporary, and I tried to believe that for about a week. But the opportunity had arisen for another gay joint to proclaim itself the city's oldest, because the Lions wasn't coming back.

This left your girlish narrator with an existential first-world problem: Where to hang out?

I checked out a few other gay bars, and they were fine, not so different from the Lions. But none were within walking distance, and my fantasies did not include getting stopped en femme for drunk driving. Of course I could have taken cabs, but I had always considered taxis so undependable that they seemed to take pride in it, and I would have been jumpy at the prospect of riding dressed with a strange driver. The prospect of adding at least twenty dollars in transport to every sissy night was also a huge buzzkill.

Gradually I came to acknowledge that there was another option, one I'd known of all along but never seriously considered. Arlin's Bar & Grill was not only right in my little slice of Clifton, it was half a block closer to home than the Lions. But Arlin's was a straight bar, which had always seemed the most foreboding of places. A place where macho culture ruled and people's behavior would be loose and unpredictable. A place where queers just didn't fit. A place to get taunted, embarrassed, and humiliated.

But times had changed since I first formed those fears, and I don't mean I had become more sanguine about queers being welcomed. What had sharply changed was society's awareness that driving didn't mix with even a slight buzz from drinking. So with the walkability issue now paramount, I had to see if Arlin's could work for me.

I had been there a few times as a guy and knew it as a mix between a watering hole for university students and an old-fashioned neighborhood tavern. I was very nervous the first few times I walked in, and one of the bartenders, a fifty-five-ish female, seemed cold and dismissive. But I was dutifully served, and on this night and others to come, I tipped generously.

Soon I was one of the regulars. The other regulars included some guys who looked mildly sketchy, but with one exception, this group mostly just let me be. Occasionally I'd see people I knew from my straight life—couples from the neighborhood or *Enquirer* photographers—but it wasn't so hard to just steer clear of those people.

The college-age crowd, however, offered occasional friendliness. I might be told how cute I looked, sometimes even by the guys in a gender-mixed crowd. I had several pairs of heels that drew comments, and one night, a girl told me that my lipstick-red skirt, with a polyurethane-shiny finish, was "just nuts, in a good way." I also remember a girl saying that a blouse with sheer polka-dot short sleeves made me look "so dainty." Priceless. I would never in my most giddy mirror sessions have thought to describe my image with that word.

The bartenders became friendly and supportive, too. When I was wearing a potentially sexy but shapeless yellow dress and confessed to a lady friend at the bar that I feared it made me look fat, a cute young barmaid interjected, "Oh, no, that dress does NOT make you look fat." How sweet of her to say that. Wearing a faux vinyl black skirt one evening, I heard one barkeep say to another, "My sister has a skirt like that, but I swear it looks better on Jackie than it does on her."

Though I still was closely hiding my real identity, I soon found myself more involved with the patrons at straight Arlin's than I ever had been at the gay Golden Lions. It wasn't so much a difference in the clientele as just a function of time. The more I dressed and went out, the less uptight I became.

These expanded interactions were of mixed quality, however.

There were morose young ladies who wanted to analyze all aspects of your transgender life. There were occasional run-ins with what I'd call an "Arlin's outlier," a moody and aggressive white-guy loner who somehow has found himself in a bar where he doesn't belong or really even want to be. Since I would be alone, this type of guy would sometimes latch onto me. A time or two I had to just leave because I couldn't shake 'em. A semiregular Hispanic guy would always tell me how great I looked, in a polite way, but he had alcohol and money problems and disappeared after a while.

Far less courtly than the Hispanic fellow was the lead singer of a band that did Arlin's gigs. I was introduced to him by a lady who had chatted me up on a couple previous visits. He was fifty-ish, projecting himself as half-cowboy/outlaw and half-hippie—a bit overweight, bearded, with a ponytail. My lady friend didn't stay long that night, and soon he was bent on getting friendlier with me.

"Do you like guys in bands, Jackie? You look to me like you do, all hotted up in that skirt and high heels. Tell you what, after this next set, let's go out to my truck and have a little smoke. I've got some really good weed out there. You like weed, don't you?"

"I do," I said. "But I had a little at home before I came up here and I really am happy to just stay here at the bar for now." I did not at all want to be confined with this dude in his personal space.

"Come on, sweetheart, you know you want to. We'll go out and be right back in. Ten minutes."

I conjured him figuring it would take exactly nine minutes and forty-five seconds for me to take two hits and then get his rocks off with a blow job.

"No," I said, beginning to feel a bit stalked. "I'm just gonna hang here a little longer and then probably head home."

"Well that sucks," he said. "But I'll be looking for you next time I'm here. Maybe you'll feel a little friendlier."

His rudeness and aggressiveness shook me. I was pissed at my lady friend for leaving me on Gross-Out Island. Worst of all, I feared he would harass me every time my visit coincided with one of his gigs. That bothered me a long time, as I'd worry before arrival about whether he'd be there. When he was, I went out of my way to avoid him, which was yet another buzzkill.

By the time I was going to Arlin's, I had developed a real photo-bug habit. I had started getting photos taken of myself in 2011, after realizing I had almost no photo evidence from forty years of my CD existence. All I had were a few Polaroid selfies from when I was about twenty-five, and seven or eight prints from a Glamour Shots photoshoot from the late '90s. But now I loved asking strangers to take photos of me in public. After taking off and putting away my femme persona, these photos would still exist in my unaccepting world. My femme identity now existed in a more durable form.

However, there was one regular who went out of his way to bully me whenever I asked people to take my photo.

"There he goes again," the asshole would holler, "getting pictures for the transvestite magazine. I hope people like his hairy back."

Only once at Arlin's did anyone make a fuss about me using the ladies' restroom. It was a woman with a very straight-seeming group who appeared to be in their late sixties or early seventies. (It's probably accurate that they were just a few years older than me, but I happily own the idea that dressing and makeup takes some years off my appearance.) This lady came into the restroom while I was washing my hands, but once she got a full load of me, she left in an obvious huff.

"What the hell is going on with fags in the women's room!" she screamed when I came out and passed their table. "It's a goddam shame for us to have to put up with that. Will somebody tell these queers to go where they're supposed to be?"

She was just venting, not addressing me directly. The others in her party were far from full-throated in support—perhaps they knew her as an obnoxious drunk—and the bar staff seemed to care not at all. I was the Arlin's regular, not her, and I was still leaving good tips. I did eschew using the women's room while the lady was still there. The men's room was fine if I just went into the stall. Me, dressed, in a small men's room, crowded with drunk guys! Another one of those things I'd thought I'd never do in a billion years.

My favorite fellow patrons of all time, at least for the one evening I knew them, were two twenty-five-ish girls—one blonde and one brunette—who approached me, all smiles, on what had been a routine weeknight visit for me.

*What have I done to merit this?* I asked myself before they could speak. Friendly encounters at Arlin's were still fewer and further between than I liked, and here were two chicks acting positively thrilled to see me.

"Hi, sorry to bother you," said the blonde. "But we're throwing a twenty-first birthday party for a guy, and we're making him do all kinds of things, sort of like an initiation."

"So we were just wondering," said the brunette, "would you come over and let us make him dance with you?"

Yeah, their wording wasn't the most personally flattering. But they seemed nice, so big damn deal about their wording. They could have said "make him dance with your hideous old pansy self" and still I'd have been all in. I flattered myself that I looked pretty good. It's an opinion I rarely fail to hold. I was in a black winter dress that showed my figure well.

"Yeah, I guess I'd be up for that," I managed to say as their bombshell exploded in my cranium.

Squeals of delight from them. Another box checked on the birthday boy's to-do list.

"Tell you what," I said, still mostly reeling. "I just need a few minutes to get ready. Lemme go out back and have a smoke, then powder my nose, and I'll be back."

More happy sounds. It was a deal. They skittered back to the party group, which was congregated around the jukebox just twenty or so feet away.

That was one good smoke, out on the Arlin's back deck. I was pumped. You better believe I checked my look with extra care in the ladies' room. I returned to my little table and waited in heavenly anticipation, figuring they'd quickly come get me.

But they didn't.

Five, ten, fifteen minutes…the party people were all engaged with one another, with nary a look back at me. I guessed that they felt it was on me to come over.

"Are we gonna do this?" I asked the blonde.

"Yeah," she said, "let's do it right now."

Up we edged toward the birthday boy. His back was to us.

"Go ahead," said Blondie, "ask him."

*What?*

"Uhh, I thought *you* were gonna *tell* him," I said.

I never asked men to dance with me. It wasn't the girly way; the man should be attracted to me by my sexy good looks. And if the guy wasn't asking, or even acting that interested, the chance of rejection seemed extremely high.

Blondie huddled with her girlfriend. Then they approached Mr. Twenty-One. Then they returned with their regrets.

"We can't get him to do it," the brunette said. "Sorry."

"No sweat," I said, "thanks for asking me anyway. I understand." What the hell else could I say?

Back at my table, I kicked myself for not volunteering immediately upon their request. It seemed my smoke and my nose-powdering had cost the project crucial momentum. But soon the two girls were back, with Birthday Boy in tow.

"Hey, I just want to apologize if I hurt your feelings or anything," he said. "Dancing just isn't my thing. I didn't mean to be rude."

"Don't think a thing of it," I said. "It's nice of you to come over."

And they were a nice crowd. I mingled a few minutes and even snapped a few photos with them.

Despite my mixed experiences at Arlin's, it was clearly the place for me to hang out, all factors considered. But if you're a cross-dresser, even in cool and funky Clifton, and you don't handle things just right, there's always the chance you could go down in a hail of gunfire on your front porch.

## CHAPTER 32

# SURRENDER AT GUNPOINT

I have a delicious, sexy feeling when I'm ready to walk up to Arlin's Bar. I often tell myself I've never looked better, and most of the time I believe it. It is such a charge to step out the front door and cover the two and a half blocks to the business strip. It's a test of how well I can walk in my heels, and usually it involves quite high heels, since a bar affords dressing options that would be a bit much for daytime at the mall. I stop on the way to smoke a cigarette on some friendly church steps, just marveling at my hottie self. That smoke is a real highlight of a sissy night.

Dangerous? Not in my experience. Most people pay no attention, and those who do tend strongly toward friendly.

But especially when I was still an NFL guy, these trips required strict caution. As briefly noted above, the place I least wanted to be seen was my own front porch. People didn't have to recognize me in the dress to recognize that a CD apparently lived in my house. Those who did know me would need little detective work to figure it out.

So the scariest parts of these walks were my first steps out of the house and the last steps returning, and the return was the more daunting of the two, as I had no control over what I'd be walking into. Prior to the outbound trip, I could peer through our big bay windows and make sure the coast was clear. Sit a minute or two if not. But if the coast wasn't clear for returning, I'd be stuck outside with some combination of 1) no place to sit, 2) sore feet from heels, 3) bad weather, and/or 4) needing to pee like crazy.

My homeward route denied me a view of the house until I turned a corner off busy Clifton Avenue, only fifty or so yards from my door. I had to step rather abruptly into the potential sight of neighbors, walkers, and people getting in and out of parked cars. I'd be all eagle eyes, hoping to spot anyone before they saw me, and that went double for any neighbors. A guy two houses beyond mine posed a particular threat, as he was regularly outside somewhat late for a bedtime smoke. This was the last fellow in the hood I wanted to get a load of me. We were friendly on the brief-chat level as neighbors, but he was a rare Republican in a neighborhood of Democrats, so I perceived him as a threat to freak out about queers. He also had some connections with the local sports scene; not a good thing for Jackie.

But this unease was simply baked into the Arlin's experience. It seemed I could manage things with proper diligence. Until I couldn't.

Rounding Clifton Avenue near midnight one Saturday, I saw with extreme dread that my next-door neighbor, a nice thirty-five-ish guy named Adam, was throwing a party. A throng of youngish folks crowded his large front porch. And in this dense neighborhood, his home really was smack next door to mine.

My distress was overlaid with feelings of foolishness, as I had foreseen such a possibility but never executed the simple way to defuse its danger. What I needed, and didn't have, was access through our detached garage, which faces a different street than our front door. A strategically stashed remote could have enabled a seamless bypass of the party. But I had never bothered to replace the unworking remotes we had. We never parked in the garage, and we got along fine just raising and lowering the door with a button inside the structure.

My oversight left me no options. I would have to just hug the shadows and shrubbery as best I could for those fifty yards to the house and then endure seconds of max potential exposure before getting inside. The odds of slipping by unnoticed seemed not at all good.

But then came a move even dumber than failing to have a remote, really one of the dumbest things I have ever done. Instead of going straight up my main steps and in the front door, I tried to pass through a side fence gate into my backyard, from where I could enter the house through the basement. This side gate had become my reentry of choice on Arlin's nights, due to my fear of being spotted on the front porch. It was easy to slip into the backyard this way under cover of darkness.

Except on this night, when it was madness. While my main front door was at least somewhat removed from the party—maybe fifteen yards—this side gate was all of fifteen *feet* from Party Central. Adam not only saw me, he darned near could have leaned out and touched me.

But he didn't recognize me en femme. To him I was just a really strange-looking person walking into the backyard of his neighbor Jack's house late at night.

"Hello?" Adam called.

But I just kept on walking into the backyard.

"Uhh, pardon me?" His tone became more assertive.

More walking away by me, which was stupid, because clearly and understandably, Adam was concerned. He was a big "look-out-for-each-other" neighbor. But I found a way to get even stupider. Because I didn't want Adam to see me go into the house through the basement, I walked away from that door and into the garage instead. Why did I think it would be better for Adam to see *that*? It wasn't as if an elaborately cross-dressed yard guy was there at midnight to grab Jack's Craftsman and mow the lawn. I just wasn't thinking at all reasonably.

I was trapped, and I had served only to heighten suspicion that I must be looking to steal something. I had no option but to exit the garage and walk back to the basement entrance, even though I knew Adam would see me. And though "safe inside" had gotten Sissy out of many scrapes over the years, including at that airport hotel in Cleveland, the term didn't apply this time.

Just as I hit the top of the stairs into the kitchen, my phone rang. It was Adam, of course, and I went into freeze mode, just as when the staff had called my hotel room in Miami. I just let it ring, not ready to concede that all of this couldn't still somehow just go away. Had I just answered the call and simply told Adam I was OK, I possibly could have gotten away with telling him nothing more. But my nonanswer proved to be the stupidest move of all, triggering CD Armageddon.

In minutes, the street outside my front door was all flashing lights. It was Miami all over again, only worse. Adam had called in a burglary, or possibly even a home invasion, and the cops were showing some no-nonsense body language, one prowling around with a big spotlight.

Realizing the jig was up, I sighed and walked onto the front porch, still fully en femme. I braced for an embarrassing conversation. But the cops were not about chatting just yet.

"Get down on your knees, get down! Down on your goddam knees NOW!"

They had started screaming before my second step onto the porch. One cop was putting me in the spotlight, and *oh my,* three others were pointing guns my way.

I didn't quite pee in my panties, though. Unsettling as this was—my first career evening having cops poised to waste me—I also had faith, borne from unearned white privilege I imagine, that they eventually would let me explain. So I muttered a sarcastic profanity to myself and went down to my nyloned knees.

"If you have a weapon throw it down! Put your hands together above your head!"

Then onto the porch they came, handcuffing me. I actually found that kind of fun, because when my hands became bound behind me, my tits stuck out in what I thought was a very girly way. Then it was into the house, where I attempted to explain how this was all just an innocent misunderstanding.

I hoped it would be easy. It wasn't. Though the cops didn't keep the cuffs on me for long, they clearly thought me too suspicious to promptly take their leave. They were reluctant to accept my male driver's license as proof of legal occupancy.

"But you saw it; you saw that I knew right where my wallet was when we came in," I said. "Right here on this hutch. How am I gonna know that if I'm a burglar?"

"All we know right now," said the lone lady cop in the group, "is that from the photo, we can't verify this as your license."

I suspected another possible reason for their doggedness: a reluctance to accept that formidable resources had been deployed in the cause of a false alarm. Then a male cop interjected, "Is there anyone in the house upstairs? We need someone to verify you belong here."

It was another of those bad dream simulations that we sissies sometimes have in real life. This could have been a hit scene on *COPS*.

Valerie, Tim, and Hannah were indeed upstairs, but I knew they wouldn't have heard a thing. Because it was summertime, and because our 1885 house had no central air conditioning, lacking even the ductwork for it, we slept in summer with bedroom doors closed and window-unit ACs buzzing.

Their blissful slumber was about to end. Never had I disturbed Valerie in a manner such as this, never had I denied her the option of "out of sight, out of mind," and oh my goodness, Tim and Hannah—would they have to testify that this strange visage was their dad?

Much as folks like to say "This is not the time to panic," this *was* the time for me.

"Ooooohhh please!" I wailed. "Yes, my wife and two kids are up there, but it's soundproof in their rooms because the ACs are running. I guarantee they don't know we're here. Do we really have to disturb them about this?"

"We're sworn to protect citizens, sir," said a cop. "That includes the people upstairs."

"But haven't I shown you what you need to see? That I knew where that license was? That it's very quiet in here? That nothing is disturbed, no evidence of illegal activity?"

"Sir, you put yourself in this position. It wasn't very smart to ignore your neighbor when he called to you and then when he called on the phone. What was he supposed to think? What were we supposed to do when he called?"

I dug deep for a hole card.

"Please, if you can consider, my kids don't know anything about me, none of this stuff, I mean."

The cops huddled, and from somewhere in the quartet, my cause gained ascendance.

"We're going to let this go now, Mr. Brennan," said the lady cop. "Be careful out there."

And they were gone. But what was Adam thinking? I had to call him immediately.

"Man, I'm really sorry," he said.

"Stop it," I said. "I'm the one who should be sorry. You did what a good neighbor should do. Forget it."

Adam didn't care that I was a CD.

"By the way," he said. "You're actually not the first cross-dresser our family has known."

Ha. Too bad I had turned the whole block upside down trying to hide information that could have been shared so much more pleasantly. The CD life in microcosm.

Had other neighbors noticed the commotion? I suspected some must have, given our street's close quarters, but no one ever asked me even the most innocent question about a disturbance. The cops at the local substation now knew about me, of course, and I worried a little about that, but they would prove to be respectful of my privacy.

The incident probably cost the city a few thousand bucks in "services" provided, and you could say it was all my fault. If I hadn't minced around in a skirt and then acted stupidly, none of it would have happened. But I'm not into blaming me. How about we blame a world that assigns such shame to my nature, for no good reason except the power trip of putting somebody down?

I didn't tell Val about the cop caper right away. I figured the news would have less impact if the incident was a week or two in the past, and when I did tell her, she mainly just rolled her eyes. She was a little worried about my being out to the police, but not at all about being out to Adam.

I didn't stop going to Arlin's. By this time, I frankly could not imagine what life would be like without this outlet for my feminine urges. But only a couple months later, I was the victim of a real crime as I attempted to return home, and this time there would be no cops around.

It was about 1:00 a.m., later than my usual return time, and I was looking forward even more than usual to getting the hell out of my heels. The crime scene was barely twenty yards from my porch, adjoining a small and well-lit parking area for the condos next door.

It was over almost before I realized what was happening. As I approached my property line, I found myself suddenly in a tug of war with what looked to be a teenager. The kid was grabbing the body of my purse, and I was hanging on by the straps. I surmise he had some experience doing this, because he seemed to know what would happen next.

Snap! The straps broke, leaving me with the short end and him with the contents. Then quick as a hiccup he was off into the night. One or two accomplices, lookouts I guess, were running with him. For them it was the perfect crime. I wasn't going to chase them in a skirt and heels, and I had no appetite for calling the District V police friends who'd warned me to be careful.

But I took some wan satisfaction in it not being much of a haul for the thieves. My losses amounted to only an aging phone, maybe ten bucks in cash, and a few cigarettes. I congratulated myself for having left my driver's license and credit cards at home, a habit I'd developed to prevent losing those items in some careless way. The phone may have had some of my girly photos on it, and I hated to lose those, but it couldn't have been many.

The snatch left me unsettled and apprehensive, however. I couldn't help pondering whether my urban neighborhood had now proven unsafe at night, especially for a lone CD in love with the limited mobility of heels. I couldn't deny that the neighborhood had a rotating cast of nonresidents whose circumstances seemed challenged. And at spots along my route, it could be relatively deserted and dark.

But I wasn't going to stop my trips—hell, no—so what was a sissy to do?

*Get pepper spray*, I eventually thought. I was initially clueless about where to get it, but I learned they had it at auto parts stores. I felt rather the wimp going into a manly auto parts store for such an item, but of course it could have been for a wife or daughter.

I toted the spray on my next few trips to the bar. Since the product seemed designed mostly for women, it was kind of fun at first. But it was also a pain. I had to hand-carry it, else it would be no help during a sudden confrontation, and though I could put it away at the bar, it didn't fit into the small and cute purses I favored. Purse space was already at a premium, what with phone, glasses, keys, cigarettes, and lighters.

So—not hard to guess—my fearfulness subsided, and my pepper spray era came to a quick close. I resumed doing my trips as I always had. I'd lived in Clifton almost fifteen years at this point, and the snatch against me was my lone brush with street crime. Nor had I seen any incidents involving other people. In the end, I didn't consider it reckless to continue.

I'll always wonder whether my purse snatcher ever perceived that I was a cross-dresser rather than a woman. We hadn't chatted about it while he was robbing me.

## CHAPTER 33

# SOMETIMES THE TWAIN SHALL MEET, UNFORTUNATELY

As my CD world opened up, I still had zero desire for my football and CD worlds to meet. There was nothing to gain and everything to lose. Home, Arlin's Bar, and the mall were the places to occasionally be a girl, and Paul Brown Stadium, known as "PBS," was the place to be absolutely and irrevocably male.

Well, *almost* absolutely and irrevocably, as I did occasionally report for football duty with pretty polished toenails under my socks.

This was not an attempt to satisfy an erotic whim or just play with fire. It was another calculated acceptance of risk, a CD "business decision," if you will. I came to work with polished toenails not to secretly excite myself, but because it was a real hassle to remove and reapply polish for every single CD night out. Having those nails good to go in advance of my next adventure was a time-saver well worth the gamble. My toenails are rather gnarly, and three coats were usually required for polish to look good.

OK, I admit it. Keeping the polish on did spark a few feelings akin to those childhood days when I'd wear garters under my jeans at home. Though I wouldn't think about it every minute or even every hour, I'd sometimes enjoy going about business—with players, coaches, ownership, or media—with a scandalous secret inside my shoes.

But still it was mostly a business decision, and the riskiest part of cute toes at work involved a must in my daily routine—my workout in the team aerobics room. I could usually schedule that at the end of my day and go straight home without ever removing my socks. But when I had to do it in the middle of a workday, I needed to shower in the staff locker room.

It wasn't too big a deal when I could remember to bring a pair of closed-toe shower shoes from home. Post-shower, I'd have a big towel ready for when the rubbers came off. I'd immediately cover my foot and then pause to see if I had enough privacy to quickly drop the towel and slide on my sock.

But I didn't always remember to bring the damn shower shoes. Why didn't I just buy a pair and leave them in the locker room? I cannot provide that answer; it's shrouded in the mystery of my own peculiar and multifaceted idiocy. It's the kind of idiocy that can lead a guy to shower with his socks half on, still covering his toes.

What a head-scratcher of a look that had to be. I don't know how I'd have answered had someone asked, "Brennan, what the hell are you doing taking a shower with your socks halfway on?" Years later, I still can't think of a plausible response.

But no one ever asked, the silence serving as a reminder to CDs that the world's interest in what we're up to usually falls short of what we might fear.

I never modeled a lipstick in front of a Bengals restroom mirror, as I had in high school, and I never wore even the most gossamer of lacy bras under my Bengals polo shirt. I was forty-one when I started with the Bengals, so by then, a secret gambit with lipstick or a bra seemed embarrassingly immature.

I told myself I must never make the careless error of showing up at work with last night's makeup still showing. Every stubborn spot had to be erased the night before. But damned if a smudged eye or pinkish lip didn't manage to occasionally survive the scrub. It was always a sick and scary feeling to notice it in a restroom mirror and wonder who else might have noticed already, and it was sicker and scarier still when I had cluelessly gone the whole day with it.

"Have you got makeup on still?" Valerie might say at home in the evening. "Please get it off and try to be more careful. I worry enough about your dressing up and your job without having to worry about you being stupid about it."

After my prostrate apology, I'd do the required cleanup and then have the rest of my evening compromised by grisly exposure scenarios for the following day. Who might have noticed and might be engaged in whispering it to others? A couple of noneventful days would allow my fear to recede, but there was always the scary prospect of it happening again.

In 2013, I put work constraints to a major test by getting my ears pierced. Though there was no way to hide it, as studs were needed around the clock for the first few weeks, I largely won a gamble that a Bengals family long accustomed to players with piercings would accept this as just a counterculture statement from a colleague already known as a left-wing outlier.

But two freelance communications guys who did contracts with the Bengals did make a big deal of it, and goddamn 'em, they were both good friends! Jon Braude and Chip Namias, former pro sports PR guys themselves, found no subject of banter more intriguing than their buddy Jack's new hardware. Even after I ceased wearing the studs to the stadium, they would jump on every half-chance to bring up my former predilection.

Were I to say, just in casual shop-talk, "I'm the only NFL PR director who gives offensive linemen full statistics credit for fumble recoveries," either of them could be counted on to reply, "Yeah, and you're also the only NFL PR director who used to wear earrings."

It was always genial enough, never baldly challenging, but their repeated inquiries made it clear they both were profoundly surprised I had let those matching and possibly queer-ish studs into my football PR work. (Remember, in the NFL, my straightness was no less implicitly assumed than my birth address of Earth.) Chip and Jon made no attempt to hide that they even talked about it between themselves when I wasn't around.

On the night Jon made perhaps his one-hundredth all-time earrings remark, I was in the stands with him at a Major League Soccer game. Suddenly exasperated, I declined a one-hundredth evasive response and gave him the nutshell version of my CD story. Did it right there in a packed Section 112 of the University of Cincinnati's Nippert Stadium.

Though it was very much a knee-jerk decision, I knew I'd be safe with Jon. Our level of trust was excellent, and our mutual testosterone vibe was at a lower level than with most of my sports-world friends. Though extended discussion was discouraged by our presence in a crowd, Jon expressed considerable surprise. I was excited to have broken some ice with a straight male friend. I promptly emailed him an early draft of this narrative, and a day later, he replied that my revelation was "mind-blowing."

"Not in a bad way," he was quick to add, "but almost unimaginable."

Another source of recurring work worry involved my fake fingernails. After I'd pry 'em off, a residue of acrylic glue would remain on my real nails. The buildup could become thick—and to me, quite noticeable—if I applied and removed two or more sets in the space of a week or so. To make matters worse, sometimes the only glue I could find in stores was a brand with a pink tint.

NASA reentry shields are no tougher than this glue when it dries. It seemed that no amount of scratching or even scraping with a pocketknife could noticeably budge it off my nails. Yes, I probably could have softened it with fifteen or twenty minutes of soaking in polish remover. But I never had the self-discipline to do that at the end of a night out, or before I left for work, and I certainly couldn't do it at my desk. So I'd just sit alone in my office, scratching ineffectually at my nails, worrying how I'd explain it should someone inquire. I figured I'd offer something about a messy household project involving Gorilla Glue, only Gorilla Glue wasn't fucking *pink*.

Did anyone ever actually notice? Probably not. Did anyone ever comment? Definitely not. But the stress had been real. Who knows how many days on this planet a closeted CD ends up forfeiting due to accumulated stress?

But despite its wearing effect, CD workplace stress was not a factor in my August 2015 decision, at age sixty-three, to plan out the end of my Bengals career. It was instead the job itself, which for all its fascination and prestige was a serious grind. Work weeks in-season averaged sixty hours, with 24/7 availability should Mike Brown or the head coach urgently need something, and the offseason was plenty busy also. I wanted weekends off, like normal people had. I wanted more than a short early-summer window for squeezing in a proper vacation. I found the allure of an NFL insider position starting to fade.

Mike Brown had told me "It's an easy job" when he hired me in 1994, but just before the '15 season opener, I told Mike I desired to work until the end of 2016 and then call it quits. Two more football seasons, with one offseason in between. Mike kindly praised me for my work, said he'd miss me, and thanked me for providing the club plenty of lead time. And as the '16 season concluded, a revamped communications staff was already in place.

It was a pretty good run for me in the sports biz. I think my peers would rank me among Cincinnati's better sports journalists over my decade (1983–93), and with the Bengals, I headed a PR department that was proud to earn three finalist berths and one win of the Pete Rozelle Award. Named for the NFL commissioner who pioneered the league's extraordinary media savviness during the '60s and '70s, the Rozelle recognizes the Pro Football Writers of America's choice as the NFL's most helpful PR staff.

My retirement sparked feature stories about me in *Cincinnati Magazine* and the *Cincinnati Business Courier*. The *Enquirer* published an op-ed that I wrote about retirement, and Geoff Hobson wrote my story for Bengals.com. Geoff was kind enough to solicit testimonials for me from head coach Marvin Lewis and quarterbacks Carson Palmer and Andy Dalton, the most gratifying being Palmer's praise that "even in the most crazy and chaotic weeks, Jack was always rock steady."

My last day with the Bengals was March 25, my birthday, in 2017. Mike had been nice enough to let me stay on until that day, when I turned sixty-five and was able to claim full pension status.

Retirement gave me more time for dressing, of course, but it also led me to conclude that, with my NFL connection no longer a factor, my biggest excuse for staying closeted had vanished.

CHAPTER 34

# SO GODDAMNED QUEER

It worked well enough, for decades, for me to live daily as a male and limit my womanly desires to the hours one might accord a major hobby. Though it truly was more than just a hobby, it never seemed worth rocking the boat of my mostly comfortable and conventional life.

I wanted to play sports and hang out with the guys. I wanted to marry a woman and father a family. I wanted to have a career in sports.

Check, check, and check. I managed that, and I speculate that the fear of upsetting a nicely managed male life has discouraged plenty of other guys from coming out as CDs. Guys like us are able to stay mostly sane and happy while hiding our girl-wannabe sides. Many other LGBTQ+ folks simply cannot have a self-respecting life without fully coming out, exposing themselves to the cruelty the world offers in deplorable abundance. Cross-dressers are somewhat shielded from that, and with a perception of having "too much to lose," we often make the decision to not lose it. The price of keeping a CD skeleton in the closet seems affordable.

Until one day for me it no longer did.

As I crossed over into retirement, I began feeling a greater need to become more genuine, unashamed, and unafraid. With no NFL career to wreck anymore, I warmed to the thought of owning a more out-front role in addressing the injustice that has rained down on queers for eons. One thing I could do, I told myself, was step from the closet, making the world just one speck more open and healthy. To the many who had done it already, and more courageously, I gave thanks for their inspiration. To those still imprisoned emotionally by shame and secrecy, I hoped my story would prove heartening.

As for my own coming out, no doubt it would have been more courageous to do so while still working in the NFL. I'll never know now exactly how it would have played out. Undoubtedly it would have done more to make folks reckon with the concept of queers among us. But I wasn't willing to risk my locker-room access and possibly get hidden away in an office assignment. I didn't want to present any public issues to an employer who had been good to me, and most overridingly, there was the simple fear factor. At younger ages, the prospect of being revealed for something as outwardly queer as cross-dressing can be just too grisly to contemplate.

So why would anyone choose to write a book such as this one? One UU church friend, a man I much esteem, reviewed an early manuscript draft and offered, "I question what is to be gained by going public with a book...what about Valerie and the rest of your family? This would seem to make life more difficult for them. Why not just live the way you want (within Valerie's comfort level) and let the chips fall where they may?"

But all my close family had already said, "Go for it," and I had my reasons. Really, although I didn't see the full scope at first, this was just the perfect thing for my retirement, this journey that began way back in November 2018 with my initial strokes on my laptop. I had a sixty-six-year-old's reduced fear level about what folks might think of me, so I could do "the right thing" in support of folks still in the closet, and—hot damn—I could exercise my foremost talent (writing) in pursuit of fame and fortune.

I use those last three words in all seriousness, because the lure of graduating from "writer" to "author" was immense. It would be my way of regaining status and relevance in a sports-and-media milieu where I once had been a bit of a big shot. This was a book that only I could write, this was the best book subject I could tackle, and should my work prove good enough to merit a slice of fame, then perhaps I'd also see some fortune falling into my bank account.

While deciding to write this book is one thing, deciding to share it was completely another. I don't hate myself, but I've come to realize I am not immune from "internalized homophobia" or "internalized sexual stigma" (ISS).

ISS is described by the organization Cultural Bridges to Justice as "the involuntary belief by lesbians and gay men that the lies, stereotypes and myths about them, delivered to everyone in a heterosexist/homophobic society, ARE TRUE." (Caps in the original.)

Getting trashed all the time from all corners, in other words, can make it virtually impossible to keep from trashing yourself.

My own ISS became more evident to me when I tried to compile a short list of people to be given copies of this book while it was still a work in progress. I desired an advance group for frank feedback, and right away I could identify a double-handful of folks to share my news with comfortably. There were family members, female friends, and gay male friends. But straight male friends? Although I had plenty, I was drawing blanks.

Confiding in a "regular guy" was absolutely the hardest kind of coming out.

Bill Koch, the former sportswriting colleague of many years who had always told me "You ain't right," is my closest friend for male bonding and just plain fun. No one approaches him as the guy whose company I most thoroughly enjoy on multiple fronts. He was the anchor of my network of sports and media friends, and because our friendship was part of this story, I could go only so far in my plans to go public without his knowledge and approval.

I felt sure that Bill liked me as much as I liked him, but I was unsure how he'd react.

Bill was a lifelong Cincinnatian, a reporter and sports columnist for many years, and later an author of successful sports books. He had much broadened himself, in my view, from a blue-collar Catholic upbringing on that conservative West Side, and we were close to lockstep with our liberal views on current affairs, as well as our avid but cynical enjoyment of sports. But there's truth to the adage about where apples fall from trees, and I sensed that cross-dressing might push the needle too far on Bill's inborn West Side weird-o-meter.

As the March equinox brought in springtime, my own internalized homophobia kicked in at max level. After letting a couple of possible "tell

Bill" days slide by, I decided on a Sunday morning in mid-April 2020 that I'd do it the next day. I promised myself repeatedly that I would not be another Paul Davenant, the protagonist in A.E. Ellis's novel *The Rack*, whose feeble procrastination on matters of vital import proves unutterably tragic.

The willies kicked in immediately Monday morning. I lingered in bed a good ninety minutes after first awakening, craving half-dozing escape. Though I normally have a healthy appetite, breakfast on this day was a no-go.

*Just get it over with,* a part of me screamed. This truly was like nothing I had experienced. But I needed a few hours to put final polish on my book synopsis, the vehicle for the tell. Upon completion of that, I would give Bill a call and alert him to my email of the synopsis. There was no real option to tell him in person, as this was in the early days of near-total COVID-19 shutdown. Nor did I want to attempt a full explanation on the phone, as that would force an immediate reaction on his part. So when I made the call about noon, I told him only that I had a book project to share with him, one that was very personal and difficult to talk about, and that he should look for my email.

Bill said he was walking the dog and that he'd check it out when they got home.

"I know what you mean about writing about personal stuff," he said. "The book I did about my dad and my relationship with him, that was difficult and a little scary at times."

Well, anyway, he *thought* he knew what I meant.

I had some yard work to do in the meantime, and I figured Bill would interrupt that with a return call by midafternoon. Then I just waited. And waited. I kept looking at the time. Midafternoon became late afternoon and early evening. *What was up with him?* I had come to know Bill as a fearlessly blunt individual, never one to shy from a frank response to anything.

He finally got back to me at seven o'clock that evening, but with only a terse and noncommittal text. He asked me to acknowledge that I'd given him "a lot to digest," and he said that as yet he had no other comment, except to express his confidence that my book would be "well-written." It was far short of the supportive response for which I'd hoped.

The next five days brought me only one additional text from Bill, also brief and enigmatic. I entered the weekend realizing that my news had roiled its recipient as much as it had roiled me to convey it. By Sunday, I still had essentially no response and was moving toward morbid worry. I poured out some angst to my Unitarian friends during a Zoom church service, but they were able to improve my mood only slightly.

In all my years of self-awareness regarding my CD nature, I had never before felt so *goddammed queer,* so dismissed and scorned by my own world. I knew I was hardly unique, that many queers before me had met that fate, but my misery wasn't assuaged by the concept of company. The late afternoon and early evening of that Sunday felt exceedingly desolate. My worst fears were coming true. Having come out—there was no going back on that now—I would have to leave behind the best parts of being a guy. Guys just wouldn't be comfortable having me around anymore.

It wasn't until 8:30 p.m., with a chill and grim spring darkness falling, when true friendship began to triumph. Bill sent me an email—an unusually lengthy one for him—with the subject line "Let People Live." That had long been one of his favorite taunts to religious-right moralizers. He acknowledged that his six days of silence must have been troubling to me. He begged my understanding that he had been "stunned" by my revelation and had needed time to sort his feelings. He said he had feared the loss of a key friendship, due to realities of which he'd never dreamed.

"When I said I knew what you meant about writing personal stuff," he wrote, "I was wrong. This isn't the same thing at all as what I did."

But he had recently lost a close friend to suicide, and he said he was determined not to lose another in just over a year. And over the course of that tense week, Bill had pushed himself to a determination that my newly updated identity did not have to fundamentally alter our relationship.

He said in his email that he still wasn't ready to talk, and it would be five more somewhat uneasy days before he broke that ice and called. We discussed my news only very briefly, and then it was on to usual subjects—the Cincinnati sports world, politics, and plans to grab lunch.

I'm still nervous to come out to more of my heterosexual friends and acquaintances. I realize that demographically, my "circles" are inevitably more queer-phobic than some. The fact that I worked in sports skews toward the conservative, and even more relevant is that folks my age were all imprinted with 1950s social conditioning. Though nobody wrote a rule about it, culture has seemed to impose that straights be naturally and effortlessly "segregated" from open queers. This segregation can spawn implicit bias, even among folks who view themselves as staunch queer allies. The segregation also feeds the stigma inside folks like me, rendering us terrified to tell otherwise good friends—especially guys— about our true natures.

Though I know rationally that it's culture's defect and not my own, it was inconceivable to me for sixty-plus years that I could ever admit to straight male friends that wearing blonde wigs excites me. As for the concept of having fun flirting with a man, well, you just don't bring this stuff up over a lunchtime gyro.

# THE CD LIFE: HALL OF FAME

This is a Cinderella story about a clingy gold tank top and how it rose to fame despite humble beginnings.

Clad in said tank during a dressed visit to Arlin's Bar, I saw an attractive young woman bouncing excitedly toward me. Such unsolicited attention came my way only rarely, and it was rarer still coming from someone as good-looking as this chick.

"I don't want to overstep any boundaries, but I've just got to tell you something if I can."

*You not only can, darling, you must.*

Nah, I wasn't near suave enough to say that. But I did bid her please continue.

"Well my girlfriend and I, we've been checking you out, and we both agree. Your boobies, seriously I'm not kidding, are about the cutest we've ever seen! They just look so good in that top. The way that fabric drapes over 'em...it's just perfect and they look so sexy. That's all, I just had to tell you. Your boobies are absolutely perfect! That top is just so great!"

And with that unimaginable compliment, that clingy top was suddenly the newest member of my "CD Hall of Fame." Though the hall exists only in my mind, to me it's right up there with Cooperstown and Canton, a shrine to the legendary performers of a pastime.

My hall of famers are clothes, shoes, wigs, and certain makeups. I admire the excellence of the best girl-makers in the business, and as is the case with baseball and football stars, their sheer talent often is accompanied by heartwarming back stories.

Some Hall of Famers seemed like losers at first but have proven themselves over time, including my white denim cutoffs with wild splotches of color all over. These shorts look like they were caught in a paintball crossfire, and I wore them at first with skepticism. But they drew compliments consistently and soon rose to the top of my heap. Everybody *loved* the colors, actually. Now these shorts never have an off day.

Other hall members have been strong from the start and then found ways to keep contributing even when their prime playing days were over. My black patent-leather stiletto pumps—Jessica Simpsons from Macy's—were my go-to hot shoes for years, never pinching and surprisingly secure to walk in. They had peep toes that made wild toenail colors pop out like crazy against their shiny blackness. These shoes are retired now from outside-the-house duty, just too worn to look great anymore, but they're still structurally sound, perfect for a little walking around the house when I just need to maintain my heel skills.

Other femme items are simply instant superstars, like the running back Jim Brown, the only rookie to ever earn NFL Most Valuable Player honors. There has never been a more surefire hall of famer from day one than the lipstick-red faux leather jacket I picked up—from Target's clearance rack—for sixteen bucks. It was amazing that they actually had one in XL, as really hot stuff often can't be found beyond size medium. The jacket has a cropped waist, extralong sleeves, and shiny silver zippers in multiple spots. For girls, to see it is to want it.

And then there's my "All-Time Roster." At the Bengals, my staff and I curated the franchise's official All-Time Player Roster, which was not for every longshot who ever signed a contract and got into a few practices. To make the official list, a player must have been in uniform and eligible to play for at least one real game.

So for my Femme Franchise, All-Time Roster status would be accorded only to items worn at least once outside the house. It may not seem a high bar, but believe me, there are plenty of clothes, shoes, and wigs in my basement that have never qualified and never will.

Some of those, unfortunately, are massive "busts," a term not related to bustlines. In football, the label of bust is slapped on a high draft choice or major trade acquisition who massively disappoints. A case in point is a pair of navy-blue stilettos with gold heels from DSW that cost me about sixty-five bucks, way more than I usually lay out. I'd never have considered them were it not for having a gift card, and they did look sexy as hell in the store. They also felt adequately comfortable. But no one at Arlin's ever remarked about them, and the gold heels just didn't show up in photos. I imagine I'll try wearing them again sometime—maybe they can rise from the ashes like the maligned Jim Plunkett did as a Super Bowl quarterback—but for now these shoes are in my doghouse.

CHAPTER 35

# COMING OUT IN *THE ATHLETIC*

**S**eptember 2020.

My tell to Bill Koch was well behind me. We had both survived it. There would not be a scarier tell down the road. I deserved a deep breath.

But not two, because I didn't have time. I had a manuscript to finish, and on a more immediate hot burner, I was scheming up a gambit so audacious it could not have been imagined even a few weeks before. As a dramatic tease to help get my book published, I would parlay my confidence from the Koch tell into the goddamned-est mass tell of all, a story about me in the national media.

The book was now an imperative. My level of investment was past where the effort could be shelved or even paused, and my fear over coming out, though still strong, was no longer all-consuming. The media story could and would be done—no backsies on this one, Sissy Girl—and it would be just the trick to separate myself from the desperate scrum of first-time authors seeking a publisher. I knew I could pull it off, because I knew scads of prominent sportswriters, and I already had my prime target in mind.

Joe Posnanski had been a pal since 1994, my first year as Bengals PR director. On the day I first met him, Joe was a talented twenty-seven-year-old, joining *The Cincinnati Post* for his first gig as a major-league city sports columnist. He looked awkward in coat-and-tie at the ultrarefined

Queen City Club, where the city's power elite regularly rubbed elbows. Lunch at the QCC was Mike Brown's way of personally welcoming Joe to the Cincy media scene.

Joe and I were both more comfortable in T-shirts, and we would go on to form a friendship that transcended our PR/media business, including numerous spirited tennis battles. Joe had left Cincinnati after just two years, headed for a bigger paper, the *Kansas City Star*, and oh my...the heights he had scaled since then were cloud-splitting.

He had become a *New York Times* bestselling author, he had copped national "Sportswriter of the Year" awards from five different organizations while working for *Sports Illustrated* and NBC, and he had won two Emmys for digital NBC Olympics coverage. And now his day job was as a star writer for the national sports website *The Athletic*, the perfect outlet for my story.

Joe was a sweetheart as well as a star. As I told him when I pitched my idea, "You are just a warm human being, interested in all sides of life and never out to put people down."

I emailed the pitch at 2:22 on a Tuesday afternoon. It was lengthy. Joe responded at 2:40. "I'm honored that you came to me with this," he said, "and I absolutely think there is great interest for it."

Within ten days Joe and I had done a pair of sixty-minute phone calls, and he had read samples of my developing manuscript. He asked me, among many other questions, if I were baring my secret for the benefit of queers still in the closet. And of course there was truth to that. How could I not hope to give some people some heart?

But the full truth was that without a book to plug, I couldn't be sure I'd have done this. I needed a reputable publisher standing behind my work, and Joe's piece would be a key in gaining that.

The story took a while coming together. It was the last days of January 2021 before we settled on a posting date of February 10. That would be Tuesday after Super Bowl LV, and our thinking was that we could capitalize on high NFL interest without getting trampled by the big game itself.

Also in late January, Joe had done me another great service.

"Have you considered," he asked, "making a list of people you want to tell about this *before* it comes out?"

I hadn't. I had been narrowly focused on what it would actually be like on posting day, when *everyone* would suddenly find out and the fallout would have to be managed, hell or high water.

But thanks to Joe it dawned that this was a stupid lack of a plan. It wasn't caring on my part, because family members and close friends who didn't yet know deserved better than an impersonal news flash. There were perhaps thirty folks who clearly deserved this heads-up, and that part was relatively easy.

"We support you 100 percent," said my older brother, Pete, a progressive in Denver with a progressive family.

"I knew you would," I said, "and I should have told you sooner. But with 1,200 miles between us, I just never found the right spot."

"The spot turned out to be now," he said. "Good luck with everything."

But just as I was feeling my bases were covered, with less than a week before posting date, I realized I still had mountains of interpersonal work to do. There had to be one hundred people or more, almost all of them guys from the NFL and sports media, with whom I was no longer in regular contact but whom I still considered friends and colleagues. How shortsighted I had been not to consider the awkwardness this could bring to future relations with any of these folks.

It wasn't that I thought anyone would feel "betrayed" or "deeply hurt" or "emotionally devastated" over not having been personally clued in. We were a bunch of guys, all right? But I wouldn't know whether everyone had 1) seen the story and liked it, 2) seen the story and disliked it, or 3) hadn't seen it at all.

If a friend had indeed seen the story, it would be unfair to burden him with whether I'd like to be contacted or would prefer a DADT silence. And if said friend had not seen it...well, I wouldn't know whether he had, and the thing would bring an elephant into the room for any future meeting, certainly for me and maybe for him.

Thus, I was committed not only to the mass coming out, but to *coming out about the coming out* in scads of personal messages. The task of simply remembering everyone was daunting.

I was properly nervous about the process but clung to faith that true friendship would prevail. Part of that faith was based on a minor tell that had spilled out of me back in July. During an ongoing group email chat among eight former Memphis sportswriters, one had made a slightly snarky remark about Caitlin Jenner. I had pushed back on that slightly, revealing nothing about myself, but darned if the next guy to respond didn't give it up that he had a transgender adult child!

His honesty and willingness to be vulnerable begat more of the same from me, and all my friends had handled it...like friends.

And so I dived in with the much larger population that still needed to be told. Scary, but doable. But how exactly would I say it? This would be, in most cases, an out-of-the-blue contact after years of little or no interaction. To a group spanning coast-to-coast, I tried it this way:

> *Hello there, old scribe and PR friends. I hope this blast email is not too impersonal. Please know that you all are meaningful friends with whom I've spent some of the best times of my life, and I've got some news for you.*
>
> *Joe Posnanski has written a story about me that is to post Feb. 10 on The Athletic. I am coming out as a lifelong cross-dresser. Part of the angle is that I may be the first male NFL "football side" team employee to come out as being on the LGBTQ spectrum. I want you to hear straight from me rather than secondhand.*
>
> *I believe that coming out is just the right thing to do, but I also hope that Poz's story will help generate interest in a book-length memoir I am completing.*
>
> *All is fine with me personally, Valerie and the rest of my family support me 100 percent.*

Versions similar to the above also went to groups of old high school pals, church people, and other various figures in my past. I sent most of them either late on February 8 or early on February 9. By midnight on February 10, my inbox had sixty-three responses.

How many were supportive? Try sixty-three. The response number would grow to 103 by week's end, and the support rate remained unanimous. Sure, some were more positive than others, and of course there were dozens more copied who didn't respond.

But the latter group, plausibly, never received it or just missed it. And as for which nonresponses could have indicated unexpressed scorn or revulsion, I barely cared. I was basking in the flood of support that just kept coming. The most common message was that true friendships are no more damaged by a cross-dressing admission than the Rockies by a rainstorm.

"My first reaction was, 'So what?'" wrote a columnist from Florida. "You're my friend. Obviously, I have a thousand questions, but I'll be whatever kind a friend you need."

Second on the frequency list—and this blew me away—were the folks who thanked me for thinking to include them.

"I'm honored that you felt comfortable enough to include me on this list," said an NFL PR colleague from Philly. "I'm honored to be in a group you trust so much."

And sportswriters, of course, are seldom short on wit.

"I hope you have more style when you dress than what I've seen from you as a guy," read a response from Dayton. "Our whole profession has a bad reputation there, so I hope you'll lift us up. But you're my pal, heels or no heels."

"We love you, Jack," said a voice from Seattle, "and now we know that at least someone has been doing something interesting during the pandemic."

Hell, some responses bordered on hero-worship:

"What you're doing takes a kind of bravery I'll never have."

"Your photo should be next to the word 'courage' in the dictionary."

"I had great respect for you before, but now it's through the roof."

I was called "rightfully beloved." And "a phenomenal human being." And a "kind soul." And of course I had "guts."

"I look forward to seeing you down the road," said a former NFL PR colleague, "and that goes for all of you."

My willingness to be vulnerable was sometimes returned in kind. One writer told me that his father had come out as gay in 1990 and he had "had no idea how to handle it." Another offered that his only child was gay. A former high school classmate revealed that he had a son who was "very confused about his sexuality" who had committed suicide at thirty-three.

And another former high school mate summed up his missive by saying, "Bottom line, this is the most uplifting message I've seen in my inbox for a long, long time."

But good as all the good wishes were, one response would stand out clearly as the most impactful. It came from Peter King, a human dynamo known by pro football fans as the "Monday Morning Quarterback" columnist at *Sports Illustrated*, among his other impressive accomplishments. Peter and I had been fiercely competitive rival Bengals beat writers in 1984, he for *The Cincinnati Enquirer* and me for the *Post*.

"I'm glad you're doing the book. It will be valuable, and it's good that you're letting people know about Joe's article in advance," Peter said in a phone conversation. "But have you thought about giving a heads-up to any of the Bengals players you spent so much time with? Like Cris and Boomer?"

He spoke of Cris Collinsworth and Boomer Esiason, standout Bengals players who both had gone on to national prominence as NFL TV analysts. I knew them both well, and hopefully vice versa, but I had always been in rather a supplicant role, they being the big-time athletes and later broadcasters, and me being the reporter or team PR director seeking their time and cooperation. It wasn't as if I'd ever had one casual beer with either of them.

And quite likely because of that—because our intercourse had always been about them and not me—I had not thought of tipping them to my reveal. The idea was intimidating, actually. Why would they care, when perhaps they had never previously known one iota about my personal life?

But when you get advice from a Peter King, you take it seriously. And Peter had a current cell number for both Boomer and Cris. Within hours, I was texting each one individually.

But, oh, was I a gutless little thing. I simply wrote, "I just want you to know that an article on me is coming out in a couple days in *The Athletic*. I'm not going to try to go into it in a text, but I didn't want you to be surprised by it."

Esiason, a proudly in-your-face Long Islander, was back at me within a half hour.

"Jack what the hell is going on here?" he texted. "What am I supposed to think about this message? Are you sick? Is your family all right? You text me but all you leave me with is some kind of mystery."

Sheepishly, I suggested that I call him to explain. And after another half hour I was borderline giddy, because Esiason had kept me on the phone for that long expressing his praise and support.

"I've got your back on this in any way I can," he concluded.

Collinsworth responded the next morning. Though more laid-back in demeanor than Esiason, he also expressed exasperation that I had texted him out of the blue—and rather ominously—without really saying shit. But from that point on, it was rinse-and-repeat, Cris offering not only affirmation but a willingness to assist.

"But what about Mike Brown?" I can hear readers asking. What of that wealthy conservative, the most significant figure in my working life for thirty-six of the previous thirty-seven years? I'd had no choice but to let Mike know early, because the Bengals held the rights to something I needed for Posnanski's story—a photo of me running onto the field with Marvin Lewis at the end of a game, barking a reminder to the coach about his media responsibilities. Far better than any other photo I had found, this one portrayed my football bona fides.

I knew that in this most unusual case, the staff who normally handled photo rights questions would feel Mike himself must be the decider. So I wrote Mike directly in his preferred medium, a snail-mail letter. After apprising him of my request to use a photo for a "story about me," I wrote in my second paragraph:

> *Mike, I am a cross-dresser, or in the vernacular of an earlier era, a "transvestite." My sexuality was evident to me as early as age three, and I have been a practicing "CD," mostly closeted of course, for most of my life since age 10 or 12.*

I stressed in my letter to Mike that Joe's story—and my book—would not portray the Bengals or the NFL in a bad light. By the point of my closing salutation, the letter ran 671 words.

I dropped it in a neighborhood box on Tuesday, January 12. I imagined Mike's response would come by letter, but I was on high alert for a possible phone call as early as midafternoon Wednesday.

I was unnervingly uncertain how he would react. I was sure he'd be courteous. Mike just always was. But my queerness figured to be on the edges of his eighty-five-year-old Republican comfort zone, and even were he not personally bothered, perhaps he would decline the photo request for business reasons, hoping to mute possible portrayal of the Bengals as involved in a culture-wars issue.

Nine anxious days passed with no response from Mike. Had the postal service fumbled the delivery? Had it arrived but been fumbled on the way to Mike's desk? Or was Mike as gobsmacked as Bill Koch had been by the news and thus in a state of nonresponse? Would I have to call him and ask if he'd received it? This was just not any fun at all.

"Here's your Mike Brown letter."

It was Valerie with the mail ten days after my letter had gone out. It was Mike expressing warm regard, if not congratulations, and approving *The Athletic*'s use of the photo. Mike even volunteered his admiration for one Jan Morris, a transgender author and historian who had climbed Mt. Everest in her days before her transition.

Further, to my considerable surprise, Mike informed me he had sought and received approval from Marvin Lewis. Here, no doubt, was the reason Mike had waited so long to respond.

My outness with the entire Bengals organization was a done deal at this point. The communications staff knew, as I had informed them I was going straight to Mike with the photo decision. The internal grapevine would complete its work with two weeks to go before my self-outing in *The Athletic*.

On February 10, the story went live. I never heard anything directly from most Bengals people, but I didn't expect that since I had not personally told anyone except Mike and the communications staff. The general public had no way to respond to the story, as *The Athletic* had disabled reader comments, but I didn't escape online trolls completely, due to a second article about me, a piece I hadn't planned.

On February 11, the *Enquirer* also covered my story, in a column by the local scene's most prominent sportswriter, Paul Daugherty. I had known "Doc"—so nicknamed because his name is pronounced "DOCK-er-tee"—since 1988, when his arrival at *The Cincinnati Post* had made us coworkers.

"I first told 'em no," Doc said when he called me on the tenth. He was referring to his editors, who had seen Posnanski's story and wanted their own version.

"I told 'em it didn't matter to me what clothes you like to wear and that it shouldn't matter to anybody else," he said. "So why should I make it a big deal by writing about it?"

"Because our culture *makes* it a big deal," I responded.

"Well, the bottom line is that the editors aren't giving up," he said, "so let's talk about this, if you want."

His column the next day treated me well, under the headline "My Friend Can Wear Whatever He Wants" and a smaller deck headline of "Jack Brennan Says He's a Cross-Dresser. So What?"

But despite its supportive content, Daugherty's column served to place me on a public hot seat for the first time. The *Enquirer* did not follow *The Athletic* in disabling reader comments, and roughly half of the thirty or so folks who chimed in were less than kind.

"So now we know Jack Brennan is a pervert," said one. "This must be very embarrassing to the Bengals and very sad for his family."

"Spare me Jack Brennan's 'intimate revelations,'" wrote another. "They make me kind of ill, frankly. Why does he have to push this at us?"

"This is supposed to be a *sports* section, not a therapy session for some weirdo," allowed a third.

I'd describe my reader experience as unsettling but not truly unnerving, and one comment by an apparently female reader brought me a wide smile.

"Paul, you had to know," she wrote, "that running a column like this would bring all the insecure men out of the woodwork."

## CHAPTER 36

# THE WRAP

I f a genie offered the chance to have lived my life as a totally straight guy, I'd decline.

But just as surely, I didn't choose this gig. I wasn't into major life decisions at three and a half. To reprise the Dr. Fred Berlin comment from the preface, "People don't choose what arouses them—they discover it."

I'll probably never know the reasons why I'm a CD, if that concept is even applicable. I just know it's a natural part of me to desire times of looking pretty and acting feminine.

For those times when I'm feeling less affirmed about my nature, I turn to more commentary from that School of Life piece on the psychology of cross-dressing.

"In truth," the essay contends, "cross-dressing is grounded in a highly logical and universal desire: the wish to be, for a time, the gender one admires, is excited by—and perhaps loves...Admiring himself in the mirror in a pair of black tights, the cross-dresser samples the intense, fascinating satisfaction of being simultaneously himself and the object of his desire."

Or to put it in more of a nutshell: I find women so overpoweringly sexy that I want to feel what it's like to be one.

To those who would say I am clinically disordered, I'd answer that we have all been conditioned to so judge. I get a dark sort of excitement from culture's avid condemnation of my nature. I can't escape—or maybe don't wish to escape—culture's maxim that queer thoughts and desires are terribly wrong.

Fortunately, I've had the support and resources to render my CD life manageable. Much as my middle-class self might scoff at those who were "born on third base and thought they hit a triple," I'll admit to having started at least on first base, and maybe on second. My inherited privileges—economic, racial, and gender-based (male)—started me on a level where a reasonably comfortable life was assured unless I screwed up quite badly. Being the kind of queer I was didn't block any of that.

No doubt, I've entertained an outsize portion of thoughts I couldn't share beyond a tiny inner circle. I've had desires that, if made public years ago, would have brought ridicule, scorn, misplaced pity, and even possibly violence.

But my actual struggles pale in comparison with the misery others have suffered for the need to be themselves. I've been lucky enough to dodge some bullets and made strong enough to withstand some glancing hits—emotional and physical. I've fallen down stairs in heels multiple times, once needing stitches for a gash on my head, and I was even hit, while clad in heels, by a slow-moving but negligent driver whom I might have avoided in regular guy shoes. I suffered a badly bruised hip. I thank goodness once again for the self-concept I developed under my parents' loving care, and I can never be thankful enough for having found Valerie. Unconditional love from my parents and spouse are the twin pillars that allowed me to keep it all together, and I know anecdotally that those pillars are far too often absent for other lipstick-loving guys, leading to lives badly damaged.

And I had access to resources that not every cross-dresser has or feels comfortable seeking out. I've attended group therapy for five years, and though I'm the only self-identified queer in the group, I once came dressed and could do it every week if I wished. I've found membership in fully inclusive church communities and have also gone to CD support groups, though I've struggled to find satisfying connections through that.

Some readers may still have suspicions about my working in close quarters with a football team for so many years, or about how Valerie managed to want to stay married to me.

As for the football part, was I sneaking peaks daily at young and sometimes naked football players, as might be expected of a sissy queer? Was I indeed a pecker checker?

My answer would be no. Despite my openness to the concept of consorting with a man as part of a CD experience, for me the Bengals locker room—and also the Reds clubhouse—were strictly workplaces. I had a living to earn in there, and personal thoughts made sense only during personal time.

An analogous situation was addressed some thirty years ago when Jim Borgman, a Pulitzer Prize–winning cartoonist for *The Cincinnati Enquirer*, took on a hot topic at the time—the admission of female journalists to football locker rooms. Arguing that women were there to do a job and not to be titillated by scantily clad men, Borgman's cartoon showed a disgusted-looking woman with a notebook amid a scene of buzzing flies, discarded athletic tape, and hairy protruding bellies. A bubble above her disgusted expression offers a sarcastic thought about what a sexy assignment she has landed. Not.

Now let's wind it up about Valerie and me as a couple. Some readers, I'm sure, are experiencing the same puzzlement expressed by one woman when I first shared my story in group therapy. "It's really hard for me to believe your wife has chosen to stay with you for forty-six years," she said, and she seemed particularly taken aback that I had not told Valerie about myself before our wedding. But I came to learn that this lady had bravely battled more than her share of pain from an ex-husband whose level of deceit and infidelity was staggering, and I know that she has since come to realize that her situation and Valerie's were not at all the same.

Also you might ask, "And the kids? Are they really all OK with this?"

All three tell me they are, even though Hannah, after reading an early manuscript, questioned my treatment of Valerie.

"Do you have regrets about how you handled it with Mom?" she asked in an email. "This is a hard one for me, because I love you so much, but the way you've written it so far definitely made me feel bad for Mom in some parts. I worry that people who don't know you will see your attitude towards Mom as insensitive."

I immediately shared Hannah's email with Valerie, who said, "Tell her it's OK. I don't think I feel hurt by any of it."

And Hannah said that was good enough for her, and my therapist even told me it was "exceptional that you could have such a frank and loving discussion with an adult child."

Valerie chose not to define our relationship on the basis of my dressing, even as she might have wished it hadn't been included in the package. Though decades were required to emerge on the other side of pervasive DADT, though I shaved my legs and kissed Ronald and otherwise took actions without "permission," choosing instead to ask forgiveness after the fact, the bedrock of our union never cracked. If Val gets all the credit for that in readers' minds, I understand that perspective, but during the forty-plus years after my confession to her in the Euless apartment bedroom, I must have shown her in some way that being her husband was still what I valued most. I didn't deceive, and I didn't choose to hide things like Ronald that I undoubtedly could have concealed, and in doing so I put our relationship first. Scoff at that if you will, but in the end it all has worked for us, and outsider views of what our "perfect" union should have been are not worthy of my concern. It hasn't been perfect for us, not even close, but at least it has been real.

"I know it's a part of you," Valerie says today, "and I love the whole you. I wouldn't want any part of you to just disappear, because if it did, you wouldn't be exactly the same person I've loved all these years. I don't know how you'd be different, but I wouldn't really want to find out."

What a woman. What a life partner. What a prize for me in life's lottery.

Though Valerie was understanding and accepting when my urges to dress led to my visiting Arlin's Bar regularly, the completion of this manuscript finds me dressing on significantly fewer days than I did in my fifties and early sixties. I am back to where I was many years ago, doing it almost exclusively when Valerie is out of town.

But it's not at all the same as in my dark-closet era. I'm not hiding from Valerie or shrinking from any extreme disapproval. It's just that I've come to strongly prefer doing my thing when I have the house to myself.

Valerie's quarterly trips to Texas to visit her mom have provided regular opportunities for me, so I shave up really well when she leaves and dress frequently during the fortnight she is away. When she's back, I'm happy enough to just let dressing go for a while. I'm not saying I have never touched my stuff between her Texas visits, but only rarely have I done the full Monty and headed out of the house.

When Valerie first discerned this altered pattern, she asked why I hadn't been dressing. She assured me she could handle it, and she hypothesized that I might be less irritable and easier to live with if I'd indulge in a few sessions. But I assured her that my reduced schedule was unrelated to any bad feelings and that I knew I could get out whenever I felt the need.

Now it's time to start managing the wider world as an avowed cross-dresser. If it makes anyone think about revealing a side of themselves that almost no one else knows, a side that makes them feel scared about being queer, all I can say is: "Come on out, please. I could use the company."

Cross-dressing will always be exciting to me, and in moments of expansive imagination, I entertain the thought of a new twist on lunch with my buddies.

*Come dressed,* they might say.

If they do, I'll be left to wrestle with a terribly important question, one that will require extensive thought and consideration:

*"What in the world am I going to wear?"*

# ACKNOWLEDGMENTS

I couldn't have pulled this off without a never-before-assembled team of all-stars who were there for me at just the right moments. Several were complete unknowns to me as the process began, so say something for serendipity.

Early on, when it still took a big gulp to break the news I was queer, my dear pal Bill Koch suggested I spill the beans to Lonnie Wheeler, a mutual friend and former sportswriting colleague who was already a major published author. Thank you, Bill, you were a bit closer to Lonnie than me, and I'm not sure I'd have thought of it myself. Lonnie was sufficiently intrigued—and kind—to flag my effort to David Black, his very influential agent. Though David would not find it a fit to represent me, he has been gracious over a long period at offering expert counsel.

It was David who suggested I contract with a professional editor to refine the manuscript, and it was Vince Vawter, another former newspaper colleague and successful author (*The Paperboy Trilogy*), who offered to "shake some trees" for me, eventually providing the name Sarah Schlick. "I don't know her," Vince said, "but a friend of mine says he's heard she's good." My first email to Ms. Schlick went unacknowledged, but who ever knows whether one email from a stranger reaches someone? I tried again, and I'm so glad I did. Sarah worked really hard for me and drove many improvements, most notably the creation of the "CD Life" inserts that appear between some chapters. Sarah's fee was so shockingly reasonable, I added a tip and suggested she raise her rates.

Then I found my own agent, but it didn't pan out, leaving me most frustrated and disappointed. Thank goodness Chip Namias was still in my corner. A former NFL PR buddy who runs his own sports business, Chip had for some time been one of my expert advisers. But his most important assist came—yes, serendipitously—when he asked if I'd be willing to share notes with another aspiring author in his circle of friends.

Holly Greenberg was writing a memoir (since published) about her father, Ed Newman, a member of the unbeaten 1972 Miami Dolphins who went on to become an esteemed judge. In about our fourth conversation, with my fuel for chasing publishers running low, Holly offered a fresh idea.

"Try university presses," she said. "They accept direct submissions, no agent required, and they'll at least give you the time of day."

Out went my proposals, the choice of destinations guided by a directory of schools' interest areas (provided by Holly). I sent to Texas and Temple and Texas Tech. To Cincinnati and Rutgers and Nebraska. To Duke and Illinois and Indiana. To Kent State and Ohio State and Oklahoma. Even to McGill-Queen's. It was no small effort, as the submission rules were different at each school.

They all, however, had the same bottom-line response: "No thanks."

But Holly had been right that I'd get some respectful feedback, and the message from Dr. Joe Schiller, acquisitions editor at Oklahoma, would prove to be the serendipity champion.

"Your project has the feel of a strong trade book (rather than a university press book)," Joe wrote. "Memoirs are notoriously tricky and hit-or-miss for us. But I wonder if Belt Publishing might be interested. They do a lot of great Midwest books, including on gender and sexuality. They have a real interest in the region, and there's potential to reach beyond that geography."

Free beer for you on your next Cincinnati trip, Joe. After reviewing a query letter, a full proposal, and the manuscript as it then stood, Belt founder and publisher Anne Trubek told me she wanted to acquire *Football Sissy*. Not long after that I heard from Belt senior editor Phoebe Mogharei, who has held my hand through the whole production process but has also held my feet to the fire. Belt likes its memoirs lean, I learned, so a lot of what Phoebe considered fat has gone up in smoke. I didn't agree with everything she proposed, and she didn't insist on everything, and in the end the manuscript feels quite fit and trim to me. Thank you, Phoebe, working with you has been a joy.

Now for some people who weren't in the serendipity chain but whose support I'll always value. Thanks to:

- My former boss Mike Brown. A conservative man in his eighties, Mike could have seen my project as not reflecting well on his football team. Instead, he graciously assisted with several key elements that only he could provide.
- My sister, Andrea O'Brien. "Kay," as she's known to close family, rode shotgun with me for every foot of this journey. She has a fabulous mind and had a world of great advice, but more than anything she was a literal soulmate, taking joy in my steps toward success as if they were her very own.
- Gary Shelton, a top-notch former sports columnist in St. Petersburg, Florida. Among the dozens of media folks who responded warmly, Gary took the most personal interest in my effort, and his engagement has helped us rekindle a great friendship.
- Doug Slagle, my former Unitarian pastor. Though not an author himself, Doug offered many sharp observations, including the reminder to my daily journalist self that authors often rework their manuscripts many times over periods of years.
- My very dearest friend Janet Ferguson of Houston. Yep, another soulmate. Exceptional personal empathy. Outstanding tips and observations.
- Lynne Lefebvre of Cincinnati, for her photo shoots of me, but mostly for her infectious joie de vivre. For reasons I can't define, Lynne has been the person with whom I felt fully comfortable ending messages with girly emojis like heels and red lips.
- The late Jon Braude, formerly PR director of the Cincinnati Reds and later an incredible contributor to Bengals PR projects. Most

of my early "tells" made me nervous. I told people only when I had to, when something from them was needed to keep the project moving. But not so with Jon. So deep was my trust level with Jon, so kind to the bone was Jon, I told *him* because I wanted to.

- Former Bengals PR staffer Ingrid "Inky" Moore, for being my No. 1 cheerleader among former team colleagues. Your unwavering enthusiasm was a tonic, Inky.
- Cris Collinsworth, Boomer Esiason, Peter King, Joe Posnanski, and Phil Simms. My football celebrity "endorsers." How much stronger is this story about a queer in football with the likes of you guys in my corner? Answer: immeasurably so.

Do authors thank their entire families in acknowledgments? I've already covered Valerie in the dedication, and I've covered Kay above, but everyone in our wider family has supported me 100 percent. Perhaps that's a bit unusual for a queer coming-out story. So hooray for us.

# ABOUT THE AUTHOR

**Jack Brennan** worked forty-four years in sports. As a journalist for multiple papers in Cincinnati, including *The Cincinnati Enquirer*, he was beat writer for both a Reds World Series winner and a Bengals Super Bowl qualifier. As public relations director for the NFL Bengals, he and his staff won the 2006 Pete Rozelle Award, conferred by pro football journalists to the league's top PR staff. Brennan grew up in Dallas, where he played low-level high school football and held his own Cowboys season tickets. He is a 1973 graduate of the University of Texas and has been married fifty-one years to his wife, Valerie, with three adult children and two grandchildren. Brennan enjoys tennis and other vigorous physical activity, he is active in progressive causes, and his favorite reads are very thick histories and biographies.

beltpublishing.com